# After We Die, Then What?

## A Compendium of Near-Death Experience Research & Findings

**Joseph Cortese, Ed.D.**

After We Die,
Then What?
A Compendium of Near-Death Experience Research & Findings

Copyright © 2021
Joseph F. Cortese, Ed.D.

Cover artwork and design by Ruth Bush.

Self published in Henderson, NV

ISBN: 978-0-578-96877-3

Library of Congress Control Number: 2021916100

Printed in the USA by
Morris Publishing®
3212 E. Hwy. 30 ~ Kearney, NE 68847
800-650-7888 ~ www.morrispublishing.com

# DEDICATION

This book is dedicated in memory of
a true friend and Brother in Christ,

*Aaron Haack*

7/21/1960 ~ 7/17/2021

<u>Aaron's Life Verse is as follows:</u>

"Be anxious for nothing, but in everything by prayer and
supplication, with
thanksgiving, let your requests be made known to God; and the
peace of
God, which surpasses all understanding, will guard your hearts
and minds
through Christ Jesus." Philippians 4:6-7 NKJV

+++++++++++++++++++++++++++++++++++++++++++++++++++++

Aaron, along with my parents, brother-in-law Barry, and many of
my relatives and friends, now know the answer to the question:
After We Die, Then What?

Until our final breath is taken on this Earth, we will not know
what they know. But through near-death experiences, we can get a
hint of what awaits us on the Other Side.

Eternal rest grant unto them, O Lord, and let perpetual
Light shine upon them. May they rest in peace. Amen.

May their souls and the souls of all the faithful departed, rest
in peace. Amen.

Remember: we are all just one breath and one heartbeat
away from eternity!

# CONTENTS

# Foreword: Food for Thought

"Most assuredly, I say to you, a servant is not greater than his master, nor is he who is sent greater than he who sent him."

--John 13:16

++++++++++++++++++++++++++++++++++++++++++++++++++++++++

## Prayer of St. Francis of Assisi

Lord, make me an instrument of Your peace.
Where there is hatred, let me sow love;
Where there is injury, pardon;
Where there is doubt, faith;
Where there is despair, hope;
Where there is darkness, light;
Where there is sadness, joy.
O, Divine Master,
Grant that I may not so much seek to be consoled as to console;
To be understood as to understand;
To be loved as to love.
For it is in giving that we receive.
It is in pardoning that we are pardoned.
It is in dying that we are born to eternal life.
++++++++++++++++++++++++++++++++++++++++++++++++++++++++

"There are no rock stars at the Table of God. We are all beggars there."---Scott Worthington, November 17, 2019, Hope Church, Las Vegas, NV

++++++++++++++++++++++++++++++++++++++++++++++++++++++++

"Death is not extinguishing the light; it is only putting out the lamp because the dawn has come."

---Rabindranath Tagor

"Death is but a dream: Finding hope and meaning in life's end."

--Christopher Kerr and Corine Mardorossian

+++++++++++++++++++++++++++++++++++++++++++++++++++++++++

## Death, be not proud (Holy Sonnet 10)

Death, be not proud, though some have called thee
Mighty and dreadful, for thou are not so;
For those whom thou think'st thou dost overthrow
Die not, poor Death, nor yet canst thou kill me.
From rest and sleep, which but thy pictures be,
Much pleasure; then from thee much more must flow,
And soonest our best men with thee do go,
Rest of their bones, and soul's delivery.
Thou'art slave to fate, chance, kings, and desperate men,
And dost with poison, war, and sickness dwell,
And poppy'or charms can make us sleep as well
And better than thy stroke; why swell'st thou then?
One short sleep past, we wake eternally,
And death shall be no more; Death, thou shalt die.

--John Donne (1633)

## "Death, be not proud" -- Summary

The speaker directly addresses and personifies Death, telling it not to be arrogant just because some people find death scary and intimidating. In fact, death is neither of these things because people don't really die when death—whom the speaker pities—comes to them; nor will the speaker truly die when death arrives for him.

Comparing death to rest and sleep—which are like images of death—the speaker anticipates death to be even more pleasurable than these activities. Death represents nothing more than the resting of the body and the arrival of the soul in the afterlife.

Death is fully controlled by fate and luck, and often administered by rulers or people acting desperately. The speaker points out that death is also associated with poison, war, and illness. Drugs and magic spells are more effective than death when it comes to rest. With all this in mind, what possible reason could death have for being so puffed up with pride?

Death is nothing but a mere sleep in between people's earthly lives and the eternal afterlife, in which death can visit them no more. It is instead death—or a certain idea of death as something to be scared of—that is going to die.[1]

++++++++++++++++++++++++++++++++++++++++++++++++++++

**Do Not Go Gentle into That Good Night**

Do not go gentle into that good night,
Old age should burn and rave at close of day;
Rage, rage against the dying of the light.

Though wise men at their end know dark is right,
Because their words had forked no lightning they
Do not go gentle into that good night.

Good men, the last wave by, crying how bright
Their frail deeds might have danced in a green bay,

Rage, rage against the dying of the light.

Wild men who caught and sang the sun in flight,
And learn, too late, they grieved it on its way,
Do not go gentle into that good night.

Grave men, near death, who see with blinding sight
Blind eyes could blaze like meteors and be gay,
Rage, rage against the dying of the light.

And you, my father, there on the sad height,
Curse, bless, me now with your fierce tears, I pray.
Do not go gentle into that good night.
Rage, rage against the dying of the light.

--Dylan Thomas (1947)

---

## "Do Not Go Gentle into That Good Night" -- Summary

Don't calmly and peacefully welcome death. The elderly should passionately fight against death as their lives come to an end. Resist, resist the oncoming darkness of your death.

Smart people at the end of their lives understand that death is inevitable—but, because they haven't yet said anything startling or revolutionary, nothing powerful enough to shock the world like a bolt of lightning, refuse to peacefully accept death.

Good people, seeing the last moments of their lives pass by like a final wave, mourn the fact that they weren't able to accomplish more, because even small actions might have moved about joyously in a "green bay"—that is, could have made a difference in the world. So they resist, resist the oncoming darkness of their deaths.

Daring people who have lived in the moment and embraced life to the fullest, metaphorically catching a joyful ride across the sky on the sun, realize too late that the sun is leaving them behind, and that even they must die—but they refuse to peacefully accept death.

Serious people, about to die, realize with sudden clarity that even those who have lost their sight can, like meteors, be full of light and happiness. So they resist, resist the oncoming darkness of their deaths.

And you, dad, are close to death, as if on the peak of a mountain. Burden and gift me with your passionate emotions, I pray to you. Do not go peacefully into the welcoming night of death. Resist, resist the oncoming darkness of your death.[2]

+++++++++++++++++++++++++++++++++++++++++++++++++++++

"O Death, where is your sting?

O Hades, where is your victory?"

--1 Corinthians 15:55 NKJV

# Introduction

In 1986, Sheldon Solomon and his associates first developed the term "terror management theory."[3] They described it as a way that humans respond, behaviorally and attitudinally, to their fear of death. Indeed, we all have that inherent fear, and it definitely affects our daily lives.

This book is not an in depth study of death, thanatology, as it is dubbed, but rather an attempt to answer the age-old question: What happens after we die? Surely, we all must die, and we all will have the answer(s), eventually. But what about the evidence of the afterlife as offered by those who have survived Near Death Experiences (NDEs)?

I will examine and explain many of these experiences through the survivors, their doctors, nurses, and other witnesses. Many times I will quote those sources, and when they are clinical and medical in their terminology, I will break that down into everyday language.

Indeed, "concerns about mortality suffuse everything that we think and do, whether we are aware of it or not," says Solomon.[4] He adds, "…when people are reminded they're going to die, they work to bolster confidence in their existing worldviews. Every culture has specific ideas about what happens when one dies."[5] Although that is true, I found that there are certain commonalities in NDEs that are shared by all cultures, across all types of religions, spiritual beliefs, and practices.

Likewise, Osis and Haraldsson (1977) found that "the major features of the NDE, such as bright, saturated colors, peace, harmony, and extraordinary beauty seem to prevail regardless of whether the patient is a Christian, Hindu, Jew or Muslim. Even though Christianity is very different, in rites, beliefs and doctrines, from the other religions this seemed to have little effect on NDEs."[6]

Yet Solomon argues that "…no culture on the face of the Earth …goes to greater lengths to deny death than ours,"[7] i.e. American culture. One thing is definite: we all will die. But what will we "see" when our hearts stops beating and we have taken our final breaths on this earth? Should we be afraid of what we will "see" on the "other side"?

Once research findings are published, many scientists and doctors willingly share their information with others. My approach is to simplify and explain such information with lay people, those who may be unfamiliar with academia. That is a God-given talent for which I am grateful. I seem to find a way to break down complex materials and explain them in everyday language. That has become particularly evident to me as I verbalize learning materials in Basic English in my international classroom. Despite the fact that I should be fully retired, I find that God has assigned me to keep teaching, and explain to individuals from every corner of the world what it is like to communicate in common, everyday English.

Death is certainly a topic that affects us all. As we age, we may ponder this topic more and more, since every breath we take advances us one breath closer to our departure from this life and entrance into another. Consider the fact that the average person has about 50,000 thoughts per day. Of those thoughts,

---

about 80 percent are negative and synonymous with a basis in fear!

As one writer puts it: "That means that more than 80 percent of the time most of us are putting our faith in fear and negativity rather than in love and miracles"[8] AND God!

Author Shannon Kaiser asks a poignant question of all of us: "Maybe the journey of life isn't so much about becoming any one thing or accomplishing any one goal. We spend so much time trying to get 'there' and be someone we think we need to be, but what if it is about *un-becoming* every single thing that isn't really true to you so you can be who you were really meant to be in the first place?"[9]

In *The Bridge of San Luis Rey*, it is Thornton Wider who reminds us: "There is a land of the living and a land of the dead and the bridge is love, the only survival, the only meaning." Indeed, fear is the opposite of love, and vice versa!

What I have attempted to do in this book is present much of the research, theories, and exploration that has taken place, or is still taking place, in the simplest and most easy-to-understand language. Some of the leading theorists and scientists present hypotheses a bit too complex for me and the ordinary reader to comprehend. However, when you ponder and digest the volume of information that I present here, you can certainly appreciate the complexity of answering the main question I pose on the cover of this book.

Let's also explore some testimonies from those who have "been there," on The Other Side, and have returned to talk about it. And, yes, I have been there! The final conclusions you draw are entirely yours and yours alone. But it is my fervent hope that you too will see The Light!

Yes, this book is truly a compendium, a brief summary of the near-death field of knowledge, which is expanding every day.

# Chapter I

## Fear of Death: The Elephant in the Room

In a January 2019 survey, 1,220 Americans 18 years of age and older were asked, "How afraid are you of death?" Statista Research Department published the results in March of 2021. The results were as follows:

- 31 percent were somewhat afraid.
- 27 percent were not very afraid.
- 25 percent were not at all afraid.
- 11 percent were very afraid.
- 7 percent didn't know.[10]

A similar survey in November 2016 of 2,973 Americans 13 years of age and older had showed that 61 percent of them believed in survival of the soul in the afterlife.[11] Other surveys over the years have demonstrated results that are fairly the same. One such survey was a 2017 study by Chapman University, which found in its "Survey of American Fear" that 20.3 percent of people in this country are "very afraid" or "afraid" of dying.[12]

The Dying Matters Coalition's research in 2009 across parts of the United Kingdom showed that 29 percent of people have discussed their wishes about dying and 68 percent claimed to be comfortable talking about death.[13] Does that seem contradictory?

The Chairperson of that Coalition, Professor Mayur Lakhani, suggested: "As a practicing GP {General Practitioner}, I know that many people feel frightened to talk about death for fear of upsetting the person they love. However, it is essential that people do not leave it until it is too late. Planning for needs and wishes helps you to be in control and helps those we leave behind."[14]

The fear of death, thanatophobia (which is derived from the Greek figure of death, Thanatos), is not recognized as an official disorder by the American Psychiatric Association (APA), although the fear often leads to general anxiety. APA has found that death anxiety peaks in a person's 20s, but that females have a secondary spike in their 50s. Humble people are less likely to be concerned about their own death.[15]

Other researchers (Kurlychek and Trenner) claim that death anxiety peaks from the ages of 40-64. It then declines in later adulthood.[16] Some have even established measuring devices for fear and death anxiety. Among those are Katenbaum and Aeinsberg, the Stroop test (used by psychologists to discover if a person in under stress due to suffering, death anxiety, or post – traumatic stress disorder (PTSD), or the Lester attitude death scale, whose validity was established in 1991.[17]

Death anxiety can lead to extreme timidity, to the point where a person may not want to discuss anything related to death at all. However, a meta-analysis study in 2016 found that lower rates of death anxiety and overall general fear of death are experienced by people who lived their religion and its practices, as compared with those who were members of a religion in name only. Other studies in international locations have found the same results, regardless of religions or practices thereof. [18]

For example, an Islamic ritual calls on people seeing a funeral procession to respectfully recognize it by stopping what they are doing and following the procession for 40 steps. Both Buddhist and Hindu religions respect the importance of death as a righteous path, instead of one of fear and anxiety.[19]

Senior editor at Guideposts, Ptolemy Tompkins, looked at the history behind other cultural beliefs and practices related to death. "The Egyptians, like the Jews and the Christians and the Muslims of later centuries, believed in physical resurrection. What this means, basically, is that they envisioned a time far in the future when the physical world and the spiritual world, which now are separate, would once again become one world."[20]

The Egyptians believed that on earth we exist as unfinished products, "but the seed of something else; a being that would emerge fully into the light only after the earthly chapter of life has ended. A being that, at least in later times, the Egyptians were not afraid to suggest was itself divine.

"In general, the fear of death can actually prove healthy for human beings. When we have a fear of dying, we often act more carefully and take appropriate precautions to minimize risks, such as wearing seat belts or bike helmets."[21]

Hollywood actor and director Woody Allen was quoted as once saying: "It's not that I'm afraid to die. I just don't want to be there when it happens," while musician Peter Tosh was quoted with: "Everybody wants to go to Heaven, but nobody wants to die."[22]

After witnessing the explosion and disintegration of the Challenger on January 28, 1986, I wondered if NASA astronauts experience a fear of death. I discovered a TED Talk with astronaut Megan McArthur, in which she said her fear of death comes from a feeling of helplessness. She remarked, "And so, over and over in my life, I've seen, of course, that training and preparation can get us ready for an event like that, but it's having the input, having the ability to impact your situation, that is what removes the fear, and balances it for you."[23] Perhaps it would be

---

wise for us, before we get launched into the next life, to properly talk about our concerns and prepare our hearts and minds without fearing the unknown, thereby impacting our situation.

"A healthy fear of death can also remind us to make the most of our time on Earth and not to take our relationships for granted. Fearing the reality of death might also push us to work harder in order to leave a lasting legacy. George Bernard Shaw summed it up best by saying, 'I want to be thoroughly used up when I die, for the harder I work the more I live,'" as noted by Angela Morrow.[24]

Shaw's quote led me to another quote, whose author, however, is unknown: "Life asked Death, 'Why do people love me but hate you?' Death responded, 'Because you are a beautiful lie and I am a painful truth.'"[25]

Yale University offers a course named "PHIL 176: Death," from which I would like to share some important quotes. In Lecture 22 – Fear of Death, Professor Shelly Kagan discusses these questions: how should the fact, and how should recognizing the fact, that we're going to die, influence how we live, and how should we respond to that fact?

Kagan states that "fear requires something bad, as the object of your fear...there's got to be a nonnegligible chance of the bad state of affairs happening, of the bad object coming to you...we need to have a certain amount of uncertainty in order to have fear be appropriate." So, for fear to make sense, you must know for certain that the bad thing is coming and how bad it is! "If you've got certainty as to the nature of the bad and certainty that it's coming, then fear doesn't make sense."

Then Kagan addresses the question: "…what are we supposedly being afraid of when we are afraid of death?" The Professor suggests that when we are afraid of death, it is really that we are afraid of being dead. More importantly, we are afraid of the distinct possibility that we will die *soon*. "It seems to me that if it weren't for the unpredictability, fear of death wouldn't make any sense at all. The only thing that it might make some sense to be afraid of is that you might die too soon—earlier rather than later. It doesn't make sense given the facts."

The fact that we all will die is truly a fact; immortality in our present physical state would be bad, with its "…eternal, dreary, dreadful existence"….says Kagan. "Anger at the fact that I'm going to die, or die too soon, doesn't make sense either."

Professor Kagan's lecture concludes with "…a kind of prayer that one of the characters in the novel {*Cat's Cradle* by Kurt Vonnegut, 1963} says—is supposed to say-at the deathbed":

God made mud.
God got lonesome.
So, God said to some of the mud, "Sit up."
"See all I've made," said God. "The hills, the sea, the sky, the stars."
And I, with some of the mud, had got to sit up and look around.
Lucky me, lucky mud.
I, mud, sat up and saw what a nice job God had done.
Nice going God!
Nobody but you could have done it God! I certainly couldn't have.
I feel very unimportant compared to You.
The only way I can feel the least bit important is to think of all the mud that didn't even get

to sit up and look around.
I got so much, and most mud got so little
Thank you for the honor!
Now mud lies down again and goes to sleep.
What memories for mud to have!
What interesting other kinds of sitting-up mud I met!
I loved everything I saw.

Kagan's final sentence in this lecture is as follows: "It seems to me that the right emotional response isn't fear, it isn't anger, it's *gratitude* that we're able to be alive at all."[26]

In Hebrews 2:14-15, Christ delivers us from the fear of death: "Inasmuch then as the children have partaken of flesh and blood, He Himself likewise shared in the same, that through death He might destroy him who had the power of death, that is, the devil, and release those who through fear of death were all their lifetime subject to bondage."

Therefore, those who believe in Christ should find "release" from the fear of death, in the hope of an eternity without their "mud," their bodies. Testifying to the terminology Vonnegut, used, "mud," please read Genesis 2:7: "And the Lord God formed man of the dust of the ground, and breathed into his nostrils the breath of life, and man became a living being."

Then, in Genesis 3:19, God re-echoes this declaration to man: "In the sweat of your face you shall eat bread till you return to the ground, for out of it you were taken; for dust you *are*, and to dust you shall return." These words are echoed every year on Quinquagesima Sunday, the Sunday which ushers in Lent, but particularly on Ash Wednesday, when many believers go to church to have ashes imposed on their foreheads in the shape of the Cross, as the following words are recited: "Remember man, that thou art dust, and unto dust thou shalt return." Those words are a translation from the Latin Mass, as celebrated in medieval times. In Latin, the exact words are "Memento, homo, quia pulvis es, et in pulverem reverteris." The ashes, by the way, symbolize humility, exaltation, death, and new life.

In the New Testament, the book of Ecclesiastes (12:5-7) seemingly echoes Genesis: "And the dust returns to the ground as it was, and the life breath returns to God Who bestowed it."

Since eighty percent of Americans die in a hospital or a nursing home, and your loved ones may not be next to you as you die, grief counselors suggest that we need to put some time into planning our end of life. We need to hear that whatever we're worried about is going to be all right. "When you believe it's okay to let go, you will."[27]

Others believe that we don't spend enough time thinking about what our fears really mean, rather than how they feel. "As we grow, we're often encouraged to think of fear as a weakness, just another childish thing to discard like baby teeth or roller skates. And I think it's no accident that we think this way. Neuroscientists have shown that human beings are hard-wired to be optimists. So maybe that's why we think of fear, sometimes, as a danger in and of itself. 'Don't worry,' we like to say to one another. 'Don't panic.' In English, fear is something we conquer. It's something we fight. It's something we overcome. But what if we looked at fear in a fresh way? What if we thought of fear as an amazing act of the imagination, something that can be profound and insightful as storytelling itself?"[28]

So, to get over our fear of death and dying, let's talk more about this "elephant in the room." Researchers also term this "elephant" a fear-death experience.[29] In countless individuals, they have observed terror of imminent death, with no signs of hope, and no other outcomes form this fear other than death itself. As we will find in this book, many times these individuals push themselves into a near-death-like (NDE) experience, with a similar pattern of aftereffects that a near-death experience offers. I view this book as my humble attempt to address the "elephant in the room." I also applaud the efforts being made by the increasing growth of Death Cafes around the world.

The first Death Café opened in England around 2011, spreading its positive, uplifting message in volunteer discussion groups. As Karen Van Dyke, host of a San Diego, CA Death Café, described the goal of these groups "is to increase awareness about death with a view to living life more fully. Once you accept death, you can truly live. There's nothing morbid about a Death Café.

"There's a big elephant in the room, and no one is paying attention to it. But at these events, you're given a safe place to talk about it, not only a safe space but a fun space. There's a sense of taking this cloak off something. That's where the magic happens…death is out of the closet."[30] She noted that attendees usually were 50 years old or older, and they tended to have some emotional connection to death, either with a relative dying or in the process of dying, on having a NDE themselves that they wanted to share with the Café.

One such NDE was that of Anita Moorjani. When she first heard of her diagnosis of cancer, she, like so many others, expressed her feelings: "Terror collided with reason. Neither Danny {Anita's husband} nor I could think. We refused to. We didn't want to think about cancer, about options, about death! I wanted to pull the normal world around me and run away.

"I was angry at the cruel joke we call life. I couldn't understand what it was all for. It seemed as though we lived for a few years; we learned from our struggles; and finally, when we got the hang of things, we ended up thrown on a fire in a wooden box. Surely, it wasn't supposed to happen so soon. It all seemed so meaningless, somehow—so pointless."[31]

Ponder the fact that a Gallup poll claimed that about eight million Americans have had a NDE![32] Another source puts it at 12-18 percent of the American population.[33] In 2019, that population totaled 328,239,523, so converting that number from percent to actual numbers would look like somewhere between 3,938, 874 and 5,908,311. My gut tells me that many people are reluctant to admit that they have experienced a NDE, simply because of our current "cancel culture" or being urged to speak in a politically correct manner, devoid of spirituality or religion. That means that the total number of Americans who have had a NDE could well number over eight million!

But what exactly is a NDE? One source defines it as "a profound experience that occurs to a person close to death or who is not near death but in a situation of physical or emotional crisis. An NDE is recounted by a person after recovery. The

NDE is characterized by a person's consciousness being forced from the physical body into an astral body. The astral body is an exact replica of the physical body, including the emotional and mental attributes, but the astral body is composed of fine nonphysical matter (subtle matter)."[34]

Until you have witnessed the funeral tradition practiced in the culture of India, as I have, you cannot imagine the grief and anguish of the family mourners as the body of their deceased loved one, placed in a wooden box, enters the fiery furnace on a conveyor belt. The mourners cling to the body and the box as long as they possibly can and follow its last journey into cremation. That scene is etched into my memory to this day, although it took place some 15 years ago. It was particularly horrific to me because the loved one was a middle school child, and I was asked, as an administrator, to be with the family through this traditional practice. Perhaps this explains why I do not favor having my body cremated. But that is another story…

Being raised in a strict Roman Catholic home, I have been present at many "viewings," or wakes, as some call them, with open and closed caskets. My own brush with death, a near-death experience, heightened my interest in researching this book and its topic. Therefore, as have so many other people who may be reading this book, I have experienced the death of my parents, my parents-in-law, and other close relatives and friends, along with many students. Some of those students died tragically and unexpectedly, either from accidents, drug overdoses, or shootings. I also have counseled students who were contemplating taking their own lives.

"According to terror management theory, fear of death is one of the most profound of human anxieties. Yet, the near-death experience and its associated pattern of after-effects represent an intriguing exception to this theory. Studies indicate the loss of the fear of death is an instantaneous and pervasive after-effect of NDEs."[35] A lecturer from Southern Methodist University, who wrote two papers on subjects related to terror management theory, maintains that we must confront our own mortality in order that we will derive meaningfulness from our lives, thereby reining in any fear of death. [36] What about the reality of fear, rather than theories about it? How do we deal with it? How is a NDE defined?

Cardiologist Pim Van Lommel wrote: "In my definition, a near-death experience (NDE) is the (reported) recollection of all the impressions gained during a special state of consciousness, which includes some specific elements such as witnessing a tunnel, a light, a panoramic life review, deceased persons, or one's own resuscitation."[37]

Van Lommel interviewed 344 consecutive patients who had been resuscitated from cardiac arrest. Of that number, 62 had experienced NDEs. All those in his research showed no EEG activity; therefore, they were classified as clinically dead.

America NDE researcher and psychiatrist Bruce Greyson defined a NDE as: "...profound psychological events with transcendental and mystical elements, typically occurring to individuals close to death or in situations of intense physical or emotional danger."[38]

---

A third person, Janice Holden, professor and former chairperson of the International Association of Near-Death Studies (IANDS), provided her definition: "...the reported memories of extreme psychological experiences with frequent 'paranormal,' transcendental, and mystical elements, which occur during a special state of consciousness arising during a period of real or imminent physical, psychological, emotional, or spiritual death, and these experiences are followed by common aftereffects."[39]

No organization has compiled more information on NDEs than NDERF, Near Death Experience Research Foundation (www.nderf.org). Each month more than 60,000 hits are made on its web site. It is the highest ranked search engine on this topic. In conjunction with IANDS, the International Association for Near-Death Studies, NDERF developed a NDE definition that goes as follows: "A lucid experience associated with perceived consciousness apart from the body occurring at the time of actual or threatened death or medical compromise." The site details over 200 NDEs in full text, and summarizes hundreds of others. I happened to browse the Media Haven section of the site, and found 22 NDE summaries that were reported in Nevada; 60 in Pennsylvania; and 284 in California, as of August, 2021. You can peruse any other states. I visited the three in which I have resided. In the Reference section of this book, it is suggested that you visit the NDERF web site for an exhaustive listing of nearly 10,000 verified, personal accounts of NDEs!

In its research, NDERF found some interesting patterns among 315 detailed NDEs:

1. 67 percent experienced difficulty in explaining their NDE;
2. Some perceived a physical and/or psychological life threatening event during the NDE;
3. Some viewed their consciousness separating from their bodies;
4. 37 percent heard and saw details of events going on around them while they were unconscious;
5. Most experienced extremely powerful and pleasant emotions;
6. Some heard distinctive sounds;
7. Many (54 percent) passed through a dark tunnel that had a bright light at its end;
8. 69 percent had an encounter with a bright light;
9. Other beings were seen by 74 percent of NDErs;
10. 35 percent were presented with a rapid life review;
11. Some visited beautiful locations during the NDE;
12. 62 percent expressed obtaining special knowledge about the universal order and/or purpose of things;
13. 44 percent encountered some type of boundary that could not be crossed if they were to return to their bodies;
14. The number of 44 was tallied again as the percentage of those who were made aware of future events;
15. NDErs were involved 62 percent of the time in making the decision to return to their bodies;
16. Often they experienced pain when they did return to their bodies;
17. Many (54 percent) reported that they had obtained paranormal or psychic abilities following their NDE;
18. A whopping 91 percent said they had changes in their attitudes or beliefs, with nearly all having no fear whatsoever of death.

In striking detail, Van Lommel describes 12 common elements of NDEs, as first noted in 1975 by Raymond Moody, a psychiatrist. For more detail, please read pages 17-41 of Van Lommel's book *Consciousness Beyond Life*. Briefly, the elements are listed as:

1. Ineffability of the experience;
2. A feeling of peace and quiet; the pain has gone;
3. The awareness of being dead, which is sometimes followed by a noise;
4. An out-of-body experience (OBE); people witness their own resuscitation or operation from a location above and outside their physical bodies;
5. A dark space, which only 15 percent of people experience; this ends rapidly as they are drawn almost magnetically, toward a tunnel; only 1-2 percent, of the original 15 percent, linger in the dark space and experience fright;
6. The perception of an unearthly environment, a magnificently beautiful landscape;
7. Meeting and communication with deceased persons, who are mainly relatives;
8. The perception of a brilliant light or a being of light; feeling of complete acceptance and unconditional love;
9. The panoramic life review; seeing your entire life flash before you;
10. The preview or flashing forward, witness to life yet to be lived;
11. The perception of a border, which, if crossed, limits their ability to return to their bodies;
12. The conscious return to the body, along with the realization that something greatly beautiful has been taken away from them, leading to a feeling of dire disappointment.

It is my belief that leading, renowned world mediums can help us deal with our feelings and attitudes about death and dying. As a Christian, I have been in the company of other Christians who have conducted a séance, but, in this book, more importantly, I must state that I have witnessed several mediums as they "connected" survivors with their departed ones.

Theresa Caputo, for one, believes that "…when the soul of a loved one passes, your relationship keeps going," and "…while you can't see or touch your loved ones anymore, their souls never leave you." She often talks and writes about how "Spirit" moves aside a thin translucent-like veil that separates our world from the next, allowing the energy of the departed one's souls to communicate through her as a device to calm the fears of the living.[40] That world seems like a fourth dimension, which we cannot see or experience until we pass into it without our physical bodies. If you want to see a three-dimension rendering of what she is referring to, please watch the movie *Ghost*. Or you may choose *The Flat-Liners*.

In one section of *Good Grief*, Caputo writes that we must "face the fears we face" in these words: "The best thing you can do when you notice fear in yourself is deal with it head-on; from there, it will gradually fade away. If you ignore it, hide it, or let it build up, your fear doesn't go anywhere; you are now just alone with your fear, which is when it takes on a life of its own. Your fears become bigger than they are and need to be. However, when you honestly and openly think about, identify, and verbalize what worries you—whether it's to a trusted friend or therapist, to a pastor or in prayer, to your loved one via a letter, or to yourself in a journal—then you no longer dwell on what's going on inside. Don't give fear the power to control your inner monologue—the things we tell ourselves on a daily basis are what motivate our thoughts and actions. Expose your fear, move through it. I don't have a pat answer to how you can accomplish this, because our fears are all so personal. But Spirit says that as you earnestly try to overcome fear, you will take back the paralyzing control that fear has over you, and that's half the battle."[41]

Medium James Van Praagh addresses fear in this way: "The opposite of love is fear. If there was no love, there would only be fear. Whenever there is an absence of love, it feels unnatural to us. Unfortunately, there is more fear in the world than love. It goes against everything that is natural to us as spiritual beings. If God is Love, then fear is a false god, and if we believe in fear, then we worship a false idol."[42]

Yes, fear can be a paralyzing force that prevents forward movement, keeping us stuck in the "mud" we referenced earlier! Another clairvoyant and medium, Sylvia Browne, who had a NDE when she was 42 years old, explained life on The Other Side in exquisite detail, and even co-authored a book with her "Spirit Guide," Francine. When I attended Catholic elementary school, the nuns told us that each of us has a "Guardian Angel" who accompanies us through life and death, whispering counsel and advice into our conscience, if we are willing to listen. It seems to me that a Guardian Angel is similar to Browne's "Spirit Guide." On the other hand, Caputo simply refers to this inner voice as Spirit.

---

Browne begins her chapter entitled "Death...and Then What?' with these words: "Even as a child in Catholic school I was frustrated by how vague everyone was about this 'life after death' thing. There seemed to be a general agreement that our spirits survive after our mortal bodies give out. It was the 'and then what?' part that inspired a lot of throat clearing and hazy, half-hearted answers; I often got the feeling it was the one question the nuns et al. were hoping no one would ask."[43]

I shared a similar experience of vagueness with the nuns as we studied catechism. "Do not ask any questions other than those in the catechism," we were told!

"But, Sister, should I be afraid of death? What is it really like when I die? Do I go to some pearly gates to be judged? If I am a good Catholic, can I still go to Hell?"

"Joseph, I told you to stop asking such questions. Only God knows those answers, and He's not telling." And so it went.

Mediums say otherwise, and some do offer hope that can lead to an alleviation of our fears about death and dying, especially those mediums that have been studied scientifically. One such medium is George Anderson, a New York Catholic. I had the pleasure of attending a session with him, just as I did with several others I write about in this book. Besides Caputo, I have been in the company of Anderson, Suzane Northrop, and Gary Spivey. By company, I mean "as a member of the audience in close proximity to the medium." Some claim that Anderson is the #1 medium in the world, due to scientific analysis of his "gift," and Northrup as #2. These will be discussed later as we move into the realm of near-death experiences, and clinical research into death and near-death experiences.

Browne's near-death experience afforded her much more detail about The Other Side than my brush with death. Her vivid descriptions are fascinating. As she did, I remember the tunnel, and no feelings of pain or fear. Here is her picture; more on mine, which is not as elaborate, later on.

"There is a very real tunnel, it turns out, and it doesn't drop down from the sky when our bodies die. Instead, it rises up from our own etheric substance, or energy field, angles across our body at about a twenty-degree angle, and delivers us to The Other Side, which is actually just three feet above our ground level, but in another dimension whose vibrational frequency is much higher than ours.

"As we move through the tunnel, we feel weightless, free, and more thrillingly alive than we ever felt for a moment in the finite, gravity-challenged bodies we left behind. No matter what the circumstances of our death, there's a pervasive sense of peace in the awareness that we're on our way Home, and we quickly see the legendary white light ahead of us, indescribably sacred, God's light.

"No matter where on earth we take our last breath, all tunnels lead to the same entrance to the perfect paradise of The Other Side...Waiting...to joyfully welcome us are loved ones from all our lifetimes on earth."[44] Sylvia died and entered The Other Side for the final time on November 20, 2013.

---

Her words, as we shall see, do not instill any sense of fear into the lives of those who return to earth after a near-death experience. In thousands upon thousands of accounts, from around the world, from people of all religions, occupations, and circumstances, the accounts are strikingly similar.

Another psychic/medium, Lisa Williams, describes fear as natural, and human. She says that "It's normal to fear death, especially when you've lost someone or are facing the transition yourself. Mediums and psychics are not immune from this fear of death either. You will see your friends and family members in the Afterlife, and therefore have a chance to love them once again."[45]  Like Sylvia Browne, Lisa had a NDE, passing through the Veil, as she termed it, as well as a tunnel that attracted her toward a White Light. Joining her experience with that of others who have had readings with her, Lisa paints a detailed picture of what life is like on The Other Side.

The "veil" is also mentioned by medium Hollister Rand. With over 25 years of experience, she stated: "Spirits speak of a tremendous grace at the time of death. Those of us left behind, however, may imagine how someone must have suffered during a horrific death. At the end of life, when someone is struggling to breathe, we may think that perhaps that person doesn't want to die and is fighting to stay. Instead, consider the possibility that the body is just doing what it is supposed to do—provide a living vehicle for the spirit. Once the spirit vacates that vehicle, the body can finally let go. Spirits will often correct our versions of their deaths to let us know that the experience wasn't how it looked, and that their passing was far easier than we envisioned."[46]

---

Rand discusses the "veil," like other experienced mediums. However, unlike others, she believes that "the veil is actually a wall of fear and anger that we have built to keep away anyone we think will continue to hurt us." She claims that spirits do not visualize our world being separated from theirs by a veil or anything else. "That is not to say that we, who are incarnate, have an all-access pass to every vibrational plane of spiritual existence. The limitations of our physical existence constrain the expansion of our consciousness. There are simply frequencies at which we can't vibrate—our physical bodies can't take it. In this sense, spirits have an advantage: they can be in more than one place at a time and can adapt to a far greater range of vibrations and frequencies. Fortunately, they're willing to retain their connections to us despite our limitations."[47]

In addition, Rand believes that we are in control of any type of veil, not spirits. She sees a veil as our own personal fear, a veil of fear as she calls it, and that we should release this barrier and "acknowledge that the love of spirits surrounds us, and they are here to guide us." In other words, we need not fear death.

"Each and every time I communicate with spirits, the evidence supports the survival of the soul." At another point, Rand exclaims, "And no way of dying separates us from love." Regarding those who have had NDEs, she says that they express disappointment at having been sent back to live longer; sometimes they are very upset and angry, perhaps dismayed, because their "surprisingly consistent Trip-Advisor-type reports grant a five-star rating to the afterlife," while Earth's is "maybe one and a half stars, with much room for improvement."[48]

So many mediums declare that there is no need to fear death or the life that awaits us in the next life. Medium James Van Praag views it this way: "I am often disappointed that a spirit's advice goes unheeded. You see, when people shed their physical bodies at death, their spiritual selves see life from a whole new perspective. It's as if they had Lasik surgery – they can finally do without their glasses and can see more clearly. Spirits understand why certain situations had to happen. They are able to recognize the value of others, even their enemies, and what they had to learn from them. They also recognize how they could have skipped certain mistakes by not letting their eyes get in the way. After crossing into the light, spirits are eager to share their newfound knowledge with the living."[49]

As far as fear and love itself, Praag explains: "If we all decided to live in love instead of fear, there would be no blame, no war, and no hurt. As we are made in the likeness of God, and God is Love, then we must strive to express our love in everything we do, say, and are.[50]

"When we banish the fear that pollutes our minds, we see how easily and readily available love is to solve all of life's problems."[51]

Finally, he exclaims, "The victory of a life well lived is measured purely by the love you have created for yourself and others on the planet."[52] In other words, the only thing we must fear is fear itself, and the only thing that endured when we leave this live and enter another is our love. Love is the binding force that holds the universe, and us, together. Yes, God is Love, and Love is God.

---

I also considered how others outside the realm of mediums looked at fear in their everyday high-risk occupations. Included in my research was the viewpoint of a Navy Seal, who wrote: "Letting go of your fear isn't an easy thing to do…it requires a tough mindset, a positive outlook, and the ability to persevere even when it seems like the deck is stacked against you.[53]

"It is nearly impossible to overstate the importance of maintaining a positive mindset when it comes to dealing with fear. Much of the doubt and uncertainty that we feel is directly related to the fact that our brains naturally gravitate toward negative and discouraging thoughts."[54]

Indeed, these words are well written, as are the words of Marie Curie, who I'd like to quote at this point: "Nothing in life is to be feared; it is only to be understood. Now is the time to understand more, so we may fear less." Certainly, I agree, and her words have guided me in this book.

Then, consider the words of the great poet, Alfred, Lord Tennyson, who wrote of death and fear: "The shell must break before the bird can fly."

Writer Erica Brown admits in the preface of her book, *Happier Endings: A Meditation on Life and Death*, that she is profoundly "afraid to death of death." Hence, she immerses herself into her work to fight against her own "subliminal fear of death."[55] She reminds us of the fact that over 107 people die per minute in the world, and that she herself was born Jewish to a child who survived the Holocaust!

_____

Brown, herself a teacher, urges that we must make death our teacher so that we can grow spiritually and acknowledge that "we cannot live forever, that we have much living and loving to do now."[56] Her book relates what she learned from her teachers, "each of whom is worth a thousand books on death. Good teachers are those who die well and show us how with their very lives."[57]

# Chapter II

## Meeting Mediums...in the Middle

Should we believe everything we hear or read? Is there any truth at all to conspiracy theories, or are they based on total lies and mistruths? What about UFOs? Any truth to them, or are all eyewitnesses to such strange sights crazy?

I ask these questions to introduce this second chapter, since I realize than many readers of what I have written so far may think I am "absolutely crazy," or that I am not a Christian because how dare I even suggest that mediums can be even partially genuine.

To be sure, there are quite a few mentions of mediums in the Bible. Here is what I found:

+++++++++++++++++++++++++++++++++++++++++++++++++++++++++

## The Mentions of Mediums in the Bible

1. "Give no regard to mediums and familiar spirits, do not seek after them to be defiled by them. I am the Lord your God."
--Leviticus 19:31.

2. "There shall not be found among you anyone who makes his son or daughter pass through the fire, or one who practices witchcraft, or a soothsayer, or one who interprets omens, or a sorcerer, or one who conjures spirits, or a medium, or a spiritist, or one who calls up the dead. For all who do these things are an abomination to the Lord, and because of these abominations the Lord your God drives them out from before you."
--Deuteronomy 18:10-12.

3. "And when they say to you, 'Seek those who are mediums and wizards, who whisper and mutter,' should not a people seek their

God? Should they seek the dead on behalf of the living?"
--Isaiah 8:19.

4. "And the person who turns to mediums and familiar spirits, to prostitute himself with them, I will set My face against that person and cut him off from his people." --Leviticus 20:6.

5. "A man or a woman who is a medium, or who has familiar spirits, shall surely be put to death; they shall stone them with stones. Their blood shall be upon them." --Leviticus 20:27.

6. Consulted by Saul in 1 Samuel 28:3-25.

7. Manasseh "…consulted spiritists and mediums. He did much evil in the sight of the Lord, to provoke Him to anger."
--2 Kings 21:6.

8. "Moreover Josiah put away those who consulted mediums and spiritists…"--2 Kings 23:24

9. "…to another the working of miracles, to another prophecy, to another discerning of spirits, to another different kinds of tongues, to another the interpretation of tongues."
--1 Corinthians 12:10

10. "If anyone thinks himself to be a prophet or spiritual, let him acknowledge that the things which I write to you are the commandments of the Lord. But if anyone is ignorant, let him be ignorant. Therefore, brethren, desire earnestly to prophesy, and do not forbid to speak with tongues. Let all things be done decently and in order." --1 Corinthians 14:37-40.

++++++++++++++++++++++++++++++++++++++++++++++++++++

# Validity/Credibility of Mediums

Therefore, should we doubt the validity of all mediums, as Dan Casey and some others do? Casey writes: "…every medium active today is a fraud. They do have one special ability: separating the grief-stricken from their money."

He cites a recent visit to his area when Theresa Caputo "showcased" her skill. Mentioning the questions and answers exchanged between Theresa and members of the audience, he discusses her tactic as an example of "cold-reading." He claims that "the medium never, NEVER, provides unprompted information. They ask questions and the victims provide the answers."[58]

He goes on to write that the reason this method is effective is "confirmation bias." This bias has the victim forgetting about all the "misses," incorrect answers or guesses made by the medium, instead of focusing only on the correct ones. Thus, the medium eventually arrives at information about the dead person and the surviving loved one who is being questioned. He implies that Caputo and Northrop, among others he names, are frauds, rip-off artists.

Casey's comments are based on his personal bias, on his personal feelings and reactions to the interactions between Caputo and her "victims," as he calls them. However, nowhere in his article does he interview any of these "victims." Had he done so, and included their comments, the investigative and journalistic piece might have been more truthful.

Rock et al. remind us that "There is a paucity of information within the literature regarding scientifically verified mediums and their experiences," and they note that the term "validity" is often "used to describe the results of *quantitative* methodologies. The term 'credibility,' conversely, is normally used to describe the extent to which the results of *qualitative* research resonate with the participants' lived experiences."[59]

No doubt there are some psychics and mediums that are scam-artists, ripping off grief-stricken "victims" and filling their own pockets with death moneys. However, that means that there are some that are real. I will share what I have learned about some of the "real" mediums, in my humble opinion, based on seeing them in person, and researching them. Therefore, I am reflecting a *qualitative* approach.

That seemingly was the approach utilized by Gary Schwartz, an esteemed Harvard-Yale psychologist, who worked hard to test mediums. In his book, *The Afterlife Experiments*, he concluded that mediums actually do communicate with the dead. "This conclusion follows from the famous principle known as Occam's Razor, according to Ray Hyman, a somewhat harsh critic of Schwartz. Hyman, a professor emeritus of psychology hailing from the University of Oregon, claims in his critique that Schwartz paraphrases Occam's principle as "All things being equal, the simpler hypothesis is usually the correct one.[60]

"As Schwartz sees it," Hyman continues, "the best experiments [supporting the reality of communicating with the dead] can be explained away, only if one makes a whole series of assumptions...These assumptions include:

---

1. that mediums use detectives to gather some of their information;
2. that sitters falsely remember specific facts such as the names of relatives;
3. that the mediums are super guessers;
4. that mediums can interpret subtle cues such as changes in breathing to infer specific details about the sitter and her relatives; and,
5. that the mediums use super telepathy to gather facts about the sitter's deceased friends and family.

"According to Schwartz, such assumptions create unnecessary complexity. 'However, if we were to apply Occam's Razor to the total set of data collected over the past hundred years, including the information you have read about in this book, there is a straightforward hypothesis that is elegant in its simplicity. This is the simple hypothesis that consciousness continues after death. This hypothesis accounts for all the data.'"[61]

Hyman's criticism centers on the fact that only five mediums were part of Schwartz's *Experiments*, and that Schwartz himself openly admitted that his *Experiments* were not ideal. The mediums often said they had erred, since they consistently came up with specific names and facts about the sitters' dead relatives and friends that were incorrect. However, Schwartz wrote that skeptics have been unable to explain these mistakes away, as cold readings, fraud, or simply lucky guesses! Since his *Experiments* were performed under very controlled and monitored situations, Schwartz believed that his mediums were genuine, as opposed to those who do cold readings or are amateur psychics.

Another reviewer of *The Afterlife Experiments* is D. J. Bem. What do his views add to our understanding at this point? Let me quote an essential paragraph from Bem's review.

As Bem writes: "Schwartz regards the cumulative findings from his experiments as compelling evidence for the afterlife hypothesis; whereas, critic Hyman regards them as totally unconvincing. My own assessment falls somewhere between these two views. I believe that the experiments do reveal evidence for some form of anomalous communication that cannot be attributed to fraud, sensory leakage, the inadequacies of subjective evaluations, or flawed statistical assessments. Despite the criticisms expressed in this review, I find sufficient support in the *quantitative* (my italics!) findings to be open to the validity...I remain unconvinced, however, that the experiments demonstrate communication with the deceased."[62] As a point of emphasis, the "I" in the above-quoted paragraph reflects the views of D. J. Bem, and not me, the author of this compendium.

### George Anderson

George is acclaimed as the world's most scientifically tested medium. He is also considered to be the world's greatest living medium, so it is only fitting that I begin with him. In 2017, I attended one of George's sessions, and I got to meet him personally.

He is not a psychic. "George is simply able to hear communication from those who have passed on, much the same way as a radio receives transmission. Unless your loved ones tell George the information they want him to relate, he does not know it. That is the very definition of a medium. Your loved ones' only interest during the session is to bring you peace and help to restore our hope through their messages."[63]

George first experienced the power of his gift of being a medium, a messenger, when he was six years old, after an illness that nearly cost him his life. He was struck with a very severe case of chicken pox, and he began to see visions of recently deceased individuals and hear their voices.

Anderson comments, "Our death is scheduled, just as our birth is," and he likes to quote Abraham Lincoln: "It's the life in your years, not the years in your life." In over 40 years of utilizing this gift, he has conducted more than 35,000 sessions with grieving survivors, and he still receives over 800 telephone calls weekly, along with more than 1,200 emails and 200 letters.

Author Joel Martin had a unique experience with George in 1980. They had never met before Joel had asked for a reading with George. George relayed specific details to Joel about the death of his late wife, Shirley. But what astounded Joel the most was George saying that Shirley had communicated a very private thing to him to prove to Joel that her spirit indeed was communicating through George. Joel could not figure out how George could repeat the phrase, "You're like a little boy." That was the phrase Shirley used whenever she was annoyed at Joel.

Martin exclaimed: "Nobody would have known that. So now I'm figuring how the heck—I could not have told that to anybody. There's no way he could've known this or should've known it. That's a very private thing."[64]

---

Shortly thereafter, Joel encouraged George to take some tests at a New York hospital, using EEGs. Half of George's brain registered inactivity and slept, while the other half "...showed normal waking patterns." The neurologist who conducted those tests said he'd never seen anything like it before. Is it what we expect to see? No. Is it what is supposed to happen. No. Is something unusual going on? Yes."[65]

In other words, when the neurologist wired-up George for analysis of his brain activity, he discovered that the right side of George's brain exhibited an unusually high level when he received information from the spirit world or from dead people. At the same time, activity on the left side of his brain, which governs the analytical, dropped significantly, was abstained from, and was pushed into the background. George described it in this way: "I have no control; I am just a telephone wire."

Anderson refers to scientists (physicists), who know that energy cannot be destroyed; it cannot die; it can only be changed in its form. Thus, our energy or life force does not die when our physical body does. As a Catholic, he sees the dust-to-dust reference, signified by placing a cross on the forehead on Ash Wednesday, as a reminder that we are creatures created by God and that we exist spirit to spirit, never having our energy, our soul, die. He says, "Energy doesn't die." Albert Einstein would certainly agree!

How does Anderson view his gift? He writes: "I have always been particularly sensitive to people who are facing end-of-life issues. I'm not exactly sure why, but I would put good money on the fact that it's because of the fear. They don't know when, they don't know how, and they wind up dying of fear just as surely as they die of their illness. My young life was filled with fear—I didn't know why the souls chose me, or why they talked, or why people here were afraid of it, or why they thought I was mentally ill. So, I understand fear. And I understand the pain that comes with fear. Nobody in the end stages of life, with everything else to worry about, should also live in fear, not knowing what kind of peace and joy awaits them."[66]

## Theresa Caputo

What does another medium, Theresa Caputo, think about the fear of death? "Most people are afraid of death. I'm not. I know I will see loved ones again and that they are around me." A passage in one of her books caught my attention in this regard: Perhaps if we forgive ourselves about our imperfections before we die, we can "…get rid of the internal guilt and shame that you might feel for what you've done. Honor that you aren't perfect, and that you're human, after all; also, if you've gone against your standards, don't slip into self-loathing. Take good care of yourself during this time; move toward self-compassion,"[67] instead of beating yourself up and dreading what awaits you on The Other Side.

Although she admits that she has never had a near-death experience or been to The Other Side, Theresa says, from her ongoing interactions with those who have lost loved ones: "When we die, our souls peacefully detach from our bodies.

---

We're greeted by the familiar souls of family and friends who died before us, and then glide toward a brilliant, eternal light that is God. On earth, we are a piece of God's energy, but in Heaven, our souls are one with His. In the physical world, I'm told that we have a primary guide—some call it a 'master guide'—who's helped us throughout our life; he or she is also there to greet us when we get to The Other Side."[68]

This, indeed, sounds very much like the near-death experience I had, and which I will write about later. It also sounds like the "Guardian Angels" the nuns taught about when I was a youngster. Yes, Theresa Caputo, like Anderson, is a Catholic, but she claims that her interactions with Spirit have nothing to do with religions. The scientists and researchers that we will look at later in this book make the same claim. They, and Caputo, say we have no reason to fear death, dying, or near-death experiences, and that NDEs are *spiritual* experiences, not religious.

Caputo continues: "Once you're free of your body, any suffering or ailment you may have felt in the physical world is immediately gone. No matter how tragic, painful, or long-suffering your death, I want to be clear that your soul detaches quickly and peacefully. Your soul may feel momentarily sad about leaving loved ones, but you're not overwhelmed with grief the way people in this world are, because your soul quickly becomes aware that you will see them again."[69]

As with George Anderson, those who have experienced Caputo's "gift," as she calls it, testify to the veracity and accuracy of the information they conveyed to the living. In their books, both mediums quote those loved ones, sometimes even using their real names, if permitted. Unlike Anderson, Caputo is much more outgoing and freely allows camera crews to tape her unplanned, spontaneous channelings, readings, conversations, between herself and the people she meets. Whether it be in a theater or auditorium, where I saw Caputo in Las Vegas, or someone in a store who just happens to be near her, Caputo receives messages from the Spirit to share information with loved ones, information that is from The Other Side. She is not reluctant to broadcast many of these interactions on a television show, *Long Island Medium*.

Concerning fear, Caputo advises: "To pursue the most positive path, which is what I try to do every day, you must really choose to meditate, pray, visualize, let go of fear, be grateful, raise your vibration, and ultimately believe that God, other Spirit, and your loved ones are around you. Their presence means that your thoughts are heard, prayers are being answered, and that miracles can unfold. I have a lot of respect for Abe Lincoln, and I've always liked when he said, 'And in the end, it's not the years in your life that count. It's the life in your years.'"[70]

I was not surprised that George Anderson recited this same Lincoln quote when I saw him in person at a small session in San Diego, CA, on August 18, 2017!

### "A River of Prayers"

Some truly gifted mediums, such as Caputo, are Christians and definitively believe, as I do, in the power of prayer. Since Caputo mentioned prayer several times in the last page or two, I think now is an appropriate time and place to include what I think is a unique viewpoint on prayer. I discovered it in Roth and Lane's *Heaven is Beyond Your Wildest Expectations: Ten True Stories of Experiencing Heaven.*

In one of those ten stories or testimonies, Dean Braxton reveals what he saw in his NDE. I will include the excerpt in its entirety for you to ponder. Braxton says that the prayers were "like shooting stars passing me. All I saw as they went by me were balls that looked like fire and a tail of light that looked like fire. I saw prayers as I was going to heaven and prayers as I was coming back to my body in the hospital on earth. I was moving in a river of prayers going to Heaven. The prayers close to me were for me; the farther away the prayers were from me, they were for other people.

"The prayers went straight to the throne and the father. Not only did they go to father God, they went inside Him…the throne of God is not a seat. It is a place. Well, more than that. He is the Throne! There were millions upon millions of prayers entering the Father. Your prayers became Him, and He became our prayers. I saw these lights of prayers like shooting stars entering the Father. I came to understand that He answers our prayers with Himself."[71]

### Suzane Northrop

Suzane's first experience with those who had died occurred when she spoke with her paternal grandmother, who had died one week earlier. She was contacted by the renowned Elizabeth Kübler-Ross in 1997 for an HBO documentary. That program explored the question of consciousness after death. The documentary later developed into *Life after Life,* in which Gary Schwartz and Linda Russek conducted research published as a book entitled *The Afterlife Experiments.*

The findings in that book claimed that Northrop and other "highly skilled mediums" were indeed legitimate in that they received their information from the "Other Side." We will look at that book a bit later. We will also look at Ray Hyman's work, *How Not to Test Mediums,* in which he severely criticized *The Afterlife Experiments.*

Suzane manages *The Suzane Northrop Radio Show*, as well as her blog on the Blog Talk Radio Network every month. She lectures and tours extensively, and it was on one such occasion that I witnessed a session in La Jolla, California, on March 10, 2017. The event was titled "Healing the Grieving Heart," and I was one of about 50 people in attendance.

She stated, "The heart is the center of where we are," and that our consciousness exists with or without our bodies. She said that we don't just become a "goody two shoes" when we die; rather our thoughts, good or bad, travel with us into the next life. Suzane mentioned *The Afterlife Experiments,* which claimed that she was one of the best mediums in the world today.

As she moved about the room, it was obvious that she was "just a telephone wire, having no control" over whom she contacted, or who contacted her. She identified people by calling out names and seeing who responded. She said that she could see only those people who have a love connection with someone in the room. She also stated that when we die, our "energy doesn't die," and that many contacts are incidental, not vivid. "Don't look for the obvious."

Claiming to be the second best medium today after George Anderson, Northrup remarked: "It's really about love. It has nothing to do with time; there is always a connection." She proceeded to recognize spirits standing near their loved ones in the room and offered consoling thoughts and personal details about their relationships while living in this world. In each case, the individuals in the room were assured that their loved ones were at peace and that they would reunite one day on The Other Side.

## Sylvia Browne: Medium or Psychic?

Browne is unique among the mediums/psychics I write about in this book, given the fact that she claimed both gifts. She was descended from a three-hundred-year psychic lineage, and she taped voices from The Other Side. She dispelled those who are non-believers, writing that they are close-minded skeptics, or they built their doubts on religious arguments. She countered: "Most of the world's great religions embrace the concept that our spirits survive death. So why is it such a bizarre thought that we can and do actually communicate with those spirits?"[72]

Before moving on, you may ask: Do psychic and mediumship abilities run in family lineages? Another medium, Hollister Rand, quips: "despite the lack of irrefutable proof that these abilities run in families, personal experiences and observations support where there is one psychic in a family, there are often more. Not only does psychic and spirit sensitivity run in my family but creativity does as well."[73]

In continuing answering the same question, Rand writes: "Generally speaking, I have found it to be true that when spirit sensitivity runs in families, it is often accompanied by a natural creativity, musical or otherwise. My extensive work with creative professionals in the entertainment industry underscores the link between creativity and psychic and spirit sensitivity. Nearly all the actors, writers, and musicians with whom I've worked acknowledge that, in their creativity, they connect with someone or something beyond themselves.

"People who don't consider themselves a creative type may say something like 'you have an amazing gift' to a medium in much the same way they would to a singer. However, using 'gift' in terms of psychic and mediumship ability is inaccurate.

"Mediumship is a talent rather than a gift. Like other talents—for instance, singing or dancing—it's something you're born to do. However, expertise in that talent is the result of learning and practice. So, when somebody says, 'I'm a natural-born medium,' that may indeed be true, but it is only half the story. Mediums are both born and made. This is why I teach mediumship—to help make it easier for others to develop their natural talent."[74]

Rand states that personal healing is also a part of becoming a medium. Unless you're in a place of healing yourself, "we can't bring people to a place of healing when we ourselves haven't been healed. I knew that there was also a link between painful childhoods and spontaneous psychic and mediumship development. It seemed to me that psychic sensitivity was a survival instinct activated to navigate life circumstances, which were often unsteady, unfathomable, and unbearable."[75]

Like some other psychics/mediums, Sylvia Browne had a near-death experience. She was undergoing routine surgery and flat-lined, at the age of forty-two. Her vision resembled that of many other people with whom she had collaborated over the years. She described a tunnel of light which rose from her body, unlike one that would lead up toward the sky. "The legendary white light appeared ahead of me, with sacred brilliance and infinite knowledge," she wrote.[76]

More than any other psychic/medium I have researched, Browne's vivid and intricate details about life on The Other Side indicated a beautiful world that defies all understanding. She explained, "Again, death is only the beginning of a whole new life, and the tunnel is simply the vehicle that delivers us there. Leaving a discussion of The Other Side with the trip through the tunnel would be like booking a fabulous journey to some exquisite locale but never asking your travel agent what, if anything, you have to look forward to after you walk off the airplane."[77]

Did Browne picture herself as a medium or a psychic? She defined a psychic as one who uses his or her gifts "…to better the human condition rather than scam or manipulate and remembering that the credit for the help they offer belongs to God, not to them."[78] Just like other psychics/mediums, she faced a great deal of disapproval as a child when her gift was displayed, being accused of being mentally disturbed. However, there is plenty of evidence to the contrary.

### Definitions: Medium or Psychic

In her book of research, based on over 10 years of study in the field with psychics and mediums, Julie Beischel defined a medium as a person who claims "…to experience regular communication with the deceased…one or a few mediumistic experiences do not make a medium…mediums are different from psychics; psychics experience regular access to information about people, the future, or distant locations they couldn't otherwise know. Mediums can also be psychic, but psychics aren't necessarily mediums. Now, what if we calmed down, put aside our assumption about how the world works, and actually applied the scientific method to the phenomenon of mediumship?"[79]

Internationally acclaimed medium and clairvoyant Lisa Williams wrote this, concerning the difference between a psychic and a medium in this way: "In a psychic reading, the reader is able to see events and situations that will happen in the future, using intuition and tapping into inner knowledge. ..we are all psychic and have access to this kind of knowledge. Some call it *women's intuition*, while others call it *inner knowledge*, but it's what happens when you're in tune with yourself and listening to your Higher Self.

"A medium, on the other hand, is the 'middleman' from one realm to the next. A medium is like a radio transmitter and the spirits are the DJs, using the medium to get their message across to the person having the reading. The medium must finely tune in, making sure to connect to the right station, so the message can be heard as clearly and accurately as possible. All mediums tend to be psychic, but psychics are rarely mediums."[80] Lisa Williams labels herself as both a psychic and a medium.

Medium James Van Praagh, who experienced a NDE, also confirms that "We are all born with some level of psychic ability. In Greek, the word *psychic* means 'of the soul.' When we use our psychic ability, we are tuning into the energy of the soul, or the natural life force that permeates every living creature."[81] Just as George Anderson describes his medium abilities as "just a telephone wire, "Van Praagh writes that he often tells a sitter that "I am merely a telephone to the spirit world."[82]

Van Praagh dedicates several pages to describing the abilities that mediums possess. In comparing his definition of medium, we find: "Those who are able to tune into the faster vibration of the spirit body after death, either in a physical or mental way, are called *sensitives* or *mediums*. As the term suggests, a medium is an individual who is a middleman or mediator, a person who goes between the spiritual and physical worlds. A medium is able to use energy to reach through the thin veil separating the physical life from the spiritual life."[83]

Medium Joseph Higgins describes mediums in this way: "Mediumship is defined as a process of communication between a person or persons from the earth plane (medium) and discarnate beings (entities without physical bodies). A medium is supposedly sensitive to vibrations from the spirit world, which enables him to communicate with discarnate entities, including guides and angels. Because of this ability, mediums can facilitate communication between spirits and people who are not mediums."[84]

His research showed that "spirits communicate messages not only about events of the past or present, but also predict future occurrences with precise accuracy. The drama in our daily lives does not interest them, as they seem to see the bigger picture of the meaning of life, which is love.[85]

"The term 'psychic' is often used as a catchall phrase for anyone who works in the paranormal. Everyone is psychic to some degree or another, but not everyone is a medium. A medium is not a fortune teller. In other words, mediums are psychics, but not all psychics are mediums. A medium works directly with a spirit, and the two have to be willing to take part in the communication process; otherwise, there is no communication."[86]

Medium Hollister Rand, who was once married to Van Praagh, defines a medium and differentiates it from a psychic and a channeler in this way: "A medium is a person who receives verifiable information from spirits and conveys messages to people in the physical world. The information is evidence that life continues beyond death, and the messages provide comfort following the loss of a loved one.

"What makes a psychic, medium, and a channeler different isn't how each receives information, but, rather, the *source* from which it is received. A psychic interprets *energy* around people, places, and things…A channeler, on the other hand, receives *messages* from one or more spirit entities (some of whom may never have lived on Earth).[87]

Another researcher into the world of mediums is Dr. Gary Schwartz, who found that mediums had an accuracy rate of 85 percent. He wrote that it was a "scientific" conclusion that the mediums he personally observed communicated with the dead, and that life after death was therefore proven. Among the mediums he tested was Suzane Northrup.

Schwartz's impressive credentials "compelled the academic world to take his findings seriously," wrote Higgins. Schwartz proclaimed: "I can no longer ignore the data and dismiss the words. They are as real as the sun, the trees and our television sets, which seem to pull pictures out of the air."[88]

Higgins details the 1993 Scole Experiment, which began in the English village of the same name, and then continued in different locations during the next six years. In that Experiment, four mediums were prompted by spirit entities "to prove that there is life beyond death and that discarnate beings from another dimension exist. The audience, in full view of these proceedings, always included NASA scientists, intellectuals, investigators of the paranormal, and other researchers. One of those who followed these sittings quite closely was Victor Zammit, an Australian lawyer and researcher of the paranormal.

Zammit called the Scole Experiment "the greatest recent afterlife experiment conducted in the Western world."[89] Overall, the Experiment was not dismissed as trickery, since professional magicians and stunt men have never been able to duplicate any of the actions observed throughout the proceedings.

Higgins cautioned: "If you are unable to make up your mind about these experiments, remember that though it is good to be a skeptic and question things, it is also important to have an open mind about phenomena that cannot be explained by mainstream science."[90]

### Gary Spivey

I never met Sylvia Browne in person. However, I did attend a "reading" held by Gary Spivey, whose occupation on Wikipedia is listed as psychic, medium, healer, cold reader, and television and talk radio personality. Gary describes himself as one with an "eccentric look," and that most definitely is true! He makes all his appearances with a huge, wide, white wig perched upon his head, and completely dressed in white from head to toe.

Spivey describes his early years in this way: "I was born spiritually gifted and could always see with my spiritual eyes (clairvoyance) and hear with my spiritual ears (clairaudience). Since becoming aware of my spiritual abilities of clairvoyance and clairaudience as a small child, I always had a sense of not being alone. I had with me what I referred to as *my pals*. My pals, as a child, were my Angels. I was lucky because my mom, Eunice, never told me that my Angels didn't exist. Whenever my pals had a story to share with her, she always listened, maybe because she was interested in what I had to say or maybe because she really loved me a lot or maybe because her dad, my grandpa Lancaster, had many of the same abilities that I have, and she knew what to expect.

"As a child, I began to demonstrate psychic abilities. I knew things before they happened; these things were usually small and unimportant, but inexplicable to a child of 4 to 5 years old. I could see things other people couldn't see."[91]

He had the same vision from his childhood years until he was in his mid-thirties. He saw a key appear before him in his dreams and meditations, a key that would fit into the earth and thereby remove any darkness, allowing the earth to glow. When he asked his Angels, who spoke to him frequently, what was meant by the vision, they always replied, "It's not time for you to understand yet. I always had a sense of missing something in my life, but I couldn't put my finger on what it was."[92]

However, it was one time when he was in his mid-thirties that Spivey said a circle of angels surrounded him as he was lying down meditating, and he heard a booming voice, which it turns out was "the *bright light* being," God. Displaying His sense of humor, God told him that He was happy he has been listening to the Angels and that Gary had kept his look as a "wooly lamb."

In the years following this episode, Spivey claimed many more conversations with God, since Gary now had the keys inside him. Those keys, or secrets, were to be shared with others to heighten their spirituality and growth as spiritual beings while on earth.

Spivey's book includes those keys, as well as many, many testimonials from individuals who experienced life changing benefits from sessions with him. On the topic of fear, Spivey writes that "It is the biggest roadblock standing in the way of accomplishing your dreams."[93] In other words, fear stops you from living your life to the fullest.

# Chapter III

## Exploring Death: The Science Behind Near-Death Experiences

I found reading about the Windbridge Institute's investigations of mediums, using scientific methods, quite fascinating. For example, Julie Beischel, a founder of that Institute, saw Assisted After-Death Communication (ADC) experiences, as a self-prescribed treatment for grief. She cited estimates that nearly one-third of American adults have had contact with the deceased. Those ADCs included: sensing the presence of the deceased loved ones; olfactory, tactile, visual, and auditory phenomena; powerful, vivid dreams; hearing music that was associated with the departed; lost-things-found; communication through electric devices; symbolic messages; synchronicities; and other phenomena that apparently defy explanation through the existing Western worldview.

These ADCs are not limited to certain types of deaths or when the deceased met their deaths; neither are they limited to any one socioeconomic group of individuals. Other researchers found that ADCs are a part of the psychological grieving needs of the surviving loved ones, and that they impact the grieving process in positive ways. All the information in this paragraph, and the previous one, is based on spontaneous ADCs. But even in the case of induced ADCs, where loved ones seek the assistance of mediums, the positive effects on the grieving process have been demonstrated.

"This extensive body of research implies a potential for similar effects after assisted ADCs, the experiences of hearing from deceased loved ones during readings with mediums."[94] In her book, Beischel listed all the scientific researchers into mediumship from the 1880s through 2013!

Regarding the media, which have recently been called "fake news" and "drive- by media" by some political conservatives and others, Beischel wrote: "But just like the media has misrepresented ADCs, it has also given the dead an undeserved bad rap: I soon learned that they (the dead) are, in fact, not scary."[95] She, along with some of the mediums she scientifically researched, concurred, stating that there is no reason to fear death, the dying, or the dead.

Beischel described her use of the scientific method in her investigation of mediumship. "Using optimal environments, maximum controls, and skilled participants, I was able to definitely conclude that certain mediums are able to report accurate and specific information about discarnates without using any normal means to acquire that information."[96]

I must admit that when I was in the audience or in the vicinity of a medium as he or she was relaying information from a "discarnate" to a live human being, I wondered how that information had been so spontaneously and anonymously obtained. Beischel suggested: "Just because we can't explain how something works doesn't mean we can't employ it as a useful element in our daily lives. At the Windbridge Institute, we care less about how mediumship works than how it can help people."[97]

The research I have done demonstrates that mediums see their gift as a way to console and strengthen others. They envision as fact that "we are first and foremost *spirits* or *souls* encapsulated in physical bodies. Our souls are the entire essence of who we are. The spirit is the ethereal or subtle body created by the soul to experience the sensations and dimensions of various realities. As a soul you can have a human experience in a physical dimension, but you must realize that this physical world is measured by the limitations of time. The spiritual dimensions, however, are not restricted by clocks, calendars, or anniversaries. To experience them, you will have to forgo 'earthly' ideas of time and open yourself to the ways of life in the world of Spirit."[98]

There are fictional stories, such as *The Five People You Meet in Heaven* by Mitch Albom, one of my favorite books. But what about all the non-fictional, true stories as documented by mediums and studied and verified by scientists, doctors, and such? Are we to believe that all these stories are fabricated, superstitious, and unbelievable?

### History of NDE Studies

The public had no specific knowledge of NDEs until Dr. Raymond Moody published his *Life After Life* in 1975. Indeed, it was Moody who first coined the term "near death experience." Moody's interest in this topic was initiated when he heard about the death experience of George Ritchie on December 20, 1943. After being dead for nine minutes, George came back to life, shocking his doctors. He described floating over his body and seeing his life flash before his eyes. A short time after he saw what he thought was an afterlife, he was told that he would not be a part of it, at that time. He came back to life and wrote a book about this experience. Later in his life, George Ritchie himself became a doctor and devoted his practice to the study of NDEs.

Years later, Moody expressed his praise of Dr. Eben Alexander's book, *Proof of Heaven: A Neurosurgeon's Journey into the Afterlife*, in this way: "Dr. Eben Alexander's near-death experience is the most astounding I have heard in more than four decades of studying this phenomenon. [He] is living proof of an afterlife."

Alexander experienced his NDE as he lay in a coma for seven days. He was suffering from a very rare brain disease, and his doctors were considering shutting down his life support. The outer surface of the brain, called the neocortex, which is the portion that makes humans human, did not function at all. After his miraculous recovery, he wrote that he had read of other NDEs, and he admitted that that "proved crucial to understanding my own journey in coma." He had no earthly memories whatsoever during his journey, "and the only pain and heartache I felt was when I had to return to earth, where I'd begun." He felt unconditional love and acceptance that defied explanation. He warned that "far too many people believe…that science and spirituality cannot coexist. They are mistaken."[99]

While in his coma, Alexander said he spent that time in heaven. "He traveled toward a white light at the end of a tunnel, saw a rolling green valley filled with flowers bursting with color, waterfalls tumbling into blue pools, revelers whirling arm in arm, and a girl who met him flying on a giant butterfly."[100]

Navy sailor Steven Musick was in a coma for five weeks, following an allergic reaction to an inoculation administered when he was a recruit. During that time, he experienced a lengthy conversation with Jesus in Heaven. He was told, "And you can't stay" by Jesus Himself, and he reentered his painful body once again, much to the shock of his hospital attendants. Thereafter, Steven suffered respiratory difficulty due to lung damage from inoculations, until one day, ten years later, at a healing service in his church.

Musick fell to the ground when an associate pastor placed his hand on Steven's chest. What happened? Steven had another NDE, in which the conversation with Jesus that he had had earlier in his life, resumed. He was back in Heaven! Jesus discussed all that Steven had experienced the past ten years, until, at one point, Jesus said, "Things will be different now." From that point on, once he regained consciousness, Steven had no more lung or respiratory issues. In fact, his physician was extremely shocked at the healthy state of Steven's lungs.

In the concluding chapter of his book, Musick answers a profound question: "What does that experience mean to me?

"We need to tell people the who of God, how he is interested, invested, gloriously obsessed with being present, with working intimately in our lives today. This is about building a relationship with the risen Christ. His presence doesn't have to wait until you die."[101]

Oprah Winfrey did a lot on her television shows to increase the knowledge that viewers had of NDEs. Dr. Jeffrey Long responded to what he called the "Oprah Factor" in this way: after surveying the same elements of NDEs before and after 1975, he found "...the content of NDEs is not influenced by prior knowledge of NDEs."[102] He cited other studies with similar results. Long studied thousands of cases, in which he saw evidence of a lucid death, wherein "consciousness leaves the body at death."

Thereby, he concluded: "I believe that having a vivid and conscious experience at the time of clinical death is among the best of evidence available to suggest a conscious existence after bodily death. It presents one of the strongest lines of evidence of the after-life."[103]

But of all this talk of consciousness, what is it exactly? Philosophers, psychiatrists, medical researchers, and scientist still grapple with its definition. "Why?" you say. Because its definition, or lack thereof, impacts any medical or scientific studies of NDEs. So, let me add one more to the collection, that of one of the greatest philosophers and psychologists who ever asked about the nature of consciousness, Franz Kafka.

In one of his journals, Kafka penned: "The meaning of life is that it stops. But that doesn't mean, as many wrongly supposed, that he felt life was pointless, irrelevant, or fated to conclude with failure (even though often enough elsewhere he was all too consumed with his own perceived personal flaws and failure). If we interpret this entry correctly it simply states something as clearly as Wiggenstein himself may have put it. Life is temporary; its chief and primal characteristic is that of impermanence. How do we intend to spend our limited time? The corollary of such an insight is even more instructive and moves us to the most obvious extension of this basic existential observation: if that is the meaning of life, its temporary condition, then what is the purpose if it?"[104]

Donald Brackett's explanation of Kafka's statement begins by Brackett writing: "The purpose of it …is to make impermanence meaningful, as in existentialism…what is meaningful is defined by the parameters, by the limits, of each individual culture and each individual occupant of that culture. This naturally suggests that all forms of meaning…are equivalent."[105] He states that each individual shares a sameness, testifying to the opposite of what we would like to believe, "…that our perspective is the right one."

Continuing on this point, Brackett writes that "…it is only our aggressively slavish perspective on this illusory condition of otherness that ever really *dies*." He offers for our consideration the myriad of reports that "…have come down to us over the ages" from all types of individuals who believe in some kind of life on the *other side* and those who have "…penetrated to …the level of consciousness and have garnered a clear picture of its continuum. They have even managed to maintain enough cognizance of their/our condition to suggest an even more spacious continuum, one extending from one life to another in a long sequence of consciousness-events fueled by a consistent source of energy, one which does not differentiate between our being a dolphin, a bee, a cactus or a Billie Holiday."[106]

### The Start of Medical and Scientific Studies of NDEs

Long's in-depth study of 613 people who had experienced a NDE detailed 12 similar elements:

1. Out-of-body experience (OBE); 75.4 percent.
2. Heightened senses; 74.4 percent.
3. Intense and generally positive emotions or feelings; 76.2 percent.
4. Passing into or through a tunnel; 33.8 percent.
5. Encountering a mystical or brilliant light; 64.6 percent.
6. Encountering other beings, either mystical beings or

deceased relatives or friends; 57.3 percent.
7. A sense of alteration of time or space; 60.5 percent.
8. Life review; 22.2 percent.
9. Encountering unworldly ("heavenly") realms; 40.6 percent.
10. Encountering or learning special knowledge; 56 percent.
11. Encountering a boundary or barrier; 31 percent.
12. A return to the body, either voluntary or involuntary; 58.5 percent.[107]

Dr. Long goes into an explanation of each of these elements and he derived nine "lines of reasoning" that proved the existence of life after death, in his opinion! If you wish to explore these in greater detail, please read his book. But for the sake of listing them briefly, they are as follows:

- It is medically inexplicable to have a highly organized and lucid experience while unconscious or clinically dead.
- NDErs may see or hear in the out-of-body (OBE) state, and what they perceive is nearly always real.
- NDEs occur during general anesthesia when no form of consciousness should be taking place.
- NDEs take place among those who are blind, and these NDEs often include visual experiences.
- A life review during the NDE accurately reflects real events in the NDEer's life, even if those events have been forgotten.

- Virtually all beings encountered during NDEs are deceased at the time of the NDE, and most are deceased relatives.
- The striking similarity of content in NDEs among very young children and that of adults strongly suggests that the content of NDEs is not due to preexisting beliefs.
- The remarkable consistency of NDEs around the world is evidence that NDEs are real events.
- NDErs are transformed in many ways by their experience, often for life.[108]

In his concluding chapter, Long reviews these same nine lines of evidence, and he writes that he is convinced that an afterlife does indeed exist. In fact, his study is the largest scientific analysis of near-death experiences, and in his final paragraph he writes: "For me personally, I'm showing more love to others now than before I started my near-death experience studies. My understanding of near-death experiences has made me a better doctor. I face life with more courage and confidence. I believe NDErs really do bring back a piece of the afterlife. When NDErs share their remarkable experiences, I believe a piece of the afterlife, in some mysterious way, becomes available to us all."[109]

This same radiation oncologist put his reputation on the line to present his finding of the Near-Death Experience Research Foundation (NDERF), which you may access at its website http://www.nderf.org/evidence. One of his most profound statements is "There is currently more scientific evidence to the reality of a near-death experience than there is for how to effectively treat certain forms of cancer."[110] I will provide more details about Long's work later in this chapter.

Earlier, we discussed the thoughts of Kafka and Brackett on the topic of consciousness that there is "something more" beyond the dead body. Allow me to add one more researcher to the discussion, Dr. Mike Sosteric. Since we are so inundated by technology, I thought it would be beneficial to include Sosteric's comparison of consciousness to the Internet! He calls the next life a Fabric of Consciousness, or a Cosmic Internet, from which "…we may 'address' and connect to, like we address and connect to a web page, certain nodes in that network.

"Death is nothing more than consciousness unplugging from an aging, antiquated, or damaged terminal, and going to find a new one. The process is simple. When the body dies, the 'soul' disconnects, the electrical activities of the terminal cease…the Cosmic Internet of which we are all a part of doesn't go away when an individual device fails. Death amounts to nothing more than a network, a reconfiguration, and I think technically a minor one at that."[111]

### Scientists and Medical Personnel Persist in "Trying" to Explain NDEs

Not everything can be explained by science or medicine. Yet there are many skeptics in both science and academia. For example, Neal Grossman, in writing the Foreword to one of Chris Carter's books, explained it in this way: "There is a hidden message in all this research, and it is a message that successful academics do not wish to hear. The message is universal love.

Every near-death experiencer is convinced that the purpose of life is to grow in our ability to give and receive love. And NDE researchers—as well as mediumship researchers—have themselves come to this same conclusion, but academic life is the opposite of loving. Many academics would be horrified to learn what all near-death experiencers have learned. A successful life is not measured by fame, prestige, wealth, or number of publications; it is measured by how we treat one another, by our ability to live according to the golden rule, and by growth in our ability to feel compassion for others."[112] After over 30 years of research, Carter's studies indicated that consciousness does not depend on the brain, and may, in fact, survive the death of our bodies.

Renowned cardiologist Dr. Pim Van Lommel is another one of those in the medical field who risked his reputation by writing about his patients' NDEs. Furthermore, he emphasized that many doctors/scientists who are skeptics, indeed, 93 percent of them, reject any form of spirituality or religion. Like Carter, Van Lommel believed that there is no beginning or no end to our consciousness, since it preceded us in birth and continues after death. Along with other medical personnel in attendance when patients experienced NDEs and then described them when they returned from the afterlife, Van Lommel viewed these experiences as a chance for all patients, their families, and physicians, nurses, etc., to lose the fear of death and try to integrate them into the rest of their collective lives.[113]

Regarding NDEs, consciousness, and the brain, cardiologist Van Lommel came to eight conclusions:

1. Many reported, to their great surprise, that they experienced an enhanced consciousness, independent of their body.
2. Current scientific knowledge cannot adequately explain the cause, nor the content of, NDEs.
3. During cardiac arrest, a lucid and enhanced consciousness can be experienced.
4. During cardiac arrest, there is scientific proof that the brain stem and cerebral cortex show no measurable activity.
5. During cardiac arrest, waking consciousness is not present.
6. Even though some scientists attempt to explain that NDEs are caused by a lack of oxygen, NDEs occur at other times when the circumstances do not threaten patients' lives.
7. Through neuroplasticity, our mind can alter brain function and anatomy.
8. Brain function and consciousness are still quite a mystery.[114]

Furthermore, Dr. Van Lommel echoed the fact that "people from all walks of life from all over the world have NDEs. The various studies found no link between the experience of a NDE and the following markers: social class, race, gender, standard of education, profession, hometown, or marital status. Prior knowledge of the existence and content of a NDE made no difference either. Researchers found no link between religion," nor the part of the world in which the NDE took place.[115]

At one time, Dr. Van Lommel emailed Dr. Sam Parnia, who was working in critical care in a hospital ER (Emergency

Room), and he shared some of the data he had just discovered. What was Parnia's reaction? "I got very excited. The researchers {Lommel et al..} had found that the occurrence of NDEs wasn't associated with the duration of cardiac arrest, unconsciousness, medication, or fear of death. Patients had then been followed for a further eight years and had been found to have undergone a transformational change in personality. Those who'd had a NDE showed a significant difference in their social and religious attitudes, as well as their attitudes toward death. They had more involvement in the family, empathy and understanding of others, less fear of death, and a more spiritual outlook on life."[116]

After looking at similar studies, Parnia raised the question: "How could thought processes, memory formation, and reasoning be occurring at a time when there was little or no brain function? Very good question! Although nearly all NDEs share common and consistent details and features, he found that "it was not the same for everyone; in fact, no two experiences were the same."[117] Yet he tried his best to be objective in his research of 2,060 patients.

Parnia concluded: "At present, however, I realized that the only aspect of NDE that was amenable to objective scientific testing was the claims of out-of-body experiences. This would help us indirectly determine if there was any possibility of a separation of mind and brain at the end of life."[118] He quoted Van Lommel: "How could a clear consciousness, outside one's body, be experienced at the moment that the brain no longer functions during a period of clinical death with flat EEG?" Basically, science has not, and it cannot, currently provide an answer. Perhaps it will be in the future, when we live in a Star Trek-type, futuristic world?

Lakhmir Chawla, a doctor from the George Washington Medical Center, specializes in palliative care for dying patients. He monitored the EEGs of his patients to spare them of any pain or to insure that they were deceased before their bodies underwent organ harvesting. What he has discovered is the fact that nearly 50 percent of these patients exhibited a very large spike in their EEG activity at the moment they died. The other half of the patients showed a flat line. Dr. Gregory Nixon in 2016 had read about this surge, and when he had the opportunity to question Chawla he did!

Nixon knew that "In humans, the surge is a coherent wave, not a seizure, which exceeds any known surge during life. This spike can last up to two minutes, which is a very long time for such intensity. For those who were previously brain-dead (no EEG activity), there was no surge at death. What this means no one is sure."[119]

Nixon also knew that Chawla had co-written an article entitled "The Quantum Soul" with Hameroff (2012), in which they described these surges as a "sort of electric catapult that helped the soul to leave the body."[120]

In his notes taken during a conference at which Chawla spoke, Nixon had the following comments regarding his questioning of Chawla: "I have to admit, I did not like the implications of immediate flat-lining, but I found the surge hopeful: at least *something* happens to many of us at death. However, the idea that an NDE could be explained by the surge (as Chawla himself once suggested) seemed wrong to me. I even got the mike and asked: 'Since an NDE is only known because the person returns to life to report it, the surge cannot be equated with the NDE, for, as you've indicated, no one comes back after the final surge, right?' He agreed but said we need more information...and so on."[121]

Along this similar line of thinking, a Canadian independent cultural journalist, writer, and curator named Donald Brackett, wrote: "Our brains don't die exactly, they merely return to the original form they had before being embodied."[122]

Parnia concluded that death is a process, during which it is entirely possible to reverse death. When he was able to get his patients' hearts, lungs, and brains back to "normal," about 40 percent of the patients who had flat lined returned to "life" and recalled elements of their NDEs.[123] They had been clinically dead before their hearts had been restarted. Noting how "consciousness continues even though the brain has completely shut down," Parnia viewed this consciousness as having some type of physicality, a "subtle force; essentially quantum consciousness."[124]

At this point, I cannot help but wonder how Parnia and Van Lommel, along with other doctors who have researched NDEs, would react to the real stories of individuals, including myself, who have experienced NDEs. As I am engaged in writing this book, I was astounded by the number of individuals who have said the following to me: "Oh, Joe, you are writing another book? What is this one about? NDEs. Oh, I had one. I saw the bright light at the end of the tunnel," as they silently drift off into a peaceful reflection of their experience. I can see it in their eyes, every time.

Or, how a relative of mine, who "died" in a nasty car accident and was pronounced DOA (Dead on Arrival) at a local hospital. All her life she had a brilliant mathematical mind, but she struggled to fit into society because of a pronounced speech impediment. Now her body lay on a refrigerated slab awaiting arrival of a family member to identify her. As the slab was pulled out, she sat up, looked at her daughter, and exclaimed "What the hell are you looking at?"

The shock on the faces in that room was intense. But now her mother was speaking with no lisp, no speech impediment whatsoever! As she was released by the astounded hospital personnel, all she could do was talk on and on about her NDE: seeing herself float away from her body in the car wreck into a tunnel of light, which became so much brighter the more she entered it. Then she saw her deceased relatives at the end of the tunnel with their hands raised, telling her, without words, telepathically, to go back. "You must return. It is not yet your time."

However, she did not want to return to her body, but almost magnetically, felt her severely damaged body pulling her backwards as she kept reaching for her departed ones. It was a very lonely feeling, she told me. She felt trapped. As I said earlier, when she returned to life on that slab that was reserved for those pronounced dead with no brain or heart activity, she never ever stuttered or stammered again. She was "dead" for quite a long time. From that point on, she became a fervent, practicing, loving Christian! Those were her personal aftereffects of her NDE experience.

None of the researchers I studied in writing this book details the psychological and physiological characteristics displayed by those who have undergone NDEs as understandably as P.M.H. Atwater does. In 80-90 percent of the cases, those who had experienced NDEs lost their fear of death, became more spiritual and less religious, with at least 11 other psychological changes in their personalities and behaviors.

As far as physiological characteristics, in the most common range of 80-95 percent of the cases, Atwater observed people who had experienced NDEs as being more sensitive to light thereafter, especially sunlight, and to sound (tastes in music change, lower blood pressure, and many, many other changes). In the quite common category of 50-79 percent of NDEs, Atwater noted reversal of the body clock, electrical sensitivity, heightened intelligence, etc. etc. You can consult p. 101 of Atwater's book for the entire list of his findings that are briefly mentioned here. The point is that all those who experienced NDEs shared similar experiences before AND after the NDE itself, although some were particularly personal and unique to the NDEer him or herself. Yes, Atwater even lists his personal changes, about 15 of them, after his three NDEs.[125]

Over 30 years, he found atheists believing in God after a NDE, young children describing a heavenly environment that they had no prior knowledge of, and many adults in the same situation, regardless of the culture or environment in which they were raised, or in which they were living when the NDE occurred. In fact, 47 percent of the adults he studied and 19 percent of children described a pleasant, heavenly experience with loving family reunions and radiant, reassuring light beings or religious figures.[126]

According to Atwater, the most common negative changes after a NDE experience included: feelings of confusion and disorientation; being disappointed with the unresponsive or uncaring attitudes of others; feelings of depression and being unable to integrate the experience into everyday life; being more uncooperative and anti-social with others; being seen as unloving and arrogant; and exhibiting the know-it-all syndrome.

On the other end of the spectrum, positive changes included: being more generous and loving; being more childlike and open-minded; displaying a heightened sense of being in the present moment; enhanced awareness of the needs of others, as well as being more creative and intuitive; having an expanded world view with less worries and fears; being more aware of their spiritual identity; and accepting and appreciating that a Higher Power exists "and that you have a role to fulfill in a Larger Plan."[127]

In his book, *Beyond the Light,* Atwater categorized all the NDEs he had researched into four different types: an initial experience in which the individual has a non-experience, leading mostly to a seed experience or an introduction to other ways to perceive reality; an unpleasant or hell-like experience; a pleasant or heaven-like experience; and a transcendent experience in which the individual is exposed to otherworldly realms and dimensions beyond their frames of references.

Atwater also noted some role reversals as a result of NDEs. Men were less willing than females to view an unpleasant or hell-like experience in a positive manner, thus striving to make good changes in their lives. More men than women reported long and rather complex descriptions of transcendent NDEs. Women, on one hand, were more assertive and outspoken, while men were more caring, thoughtful, and expressive emotionally. Note the role reversals from what one might expect from men and women in such circumstances!

Atwater's interest in NDEs was spearheaded by his own personal experiences in 1977, when he had three NDEs. Like myself, when you have the experience, you never forget it, and it has a profound effect on your life. Indeed, it does change your life. Atwater attributes the label "near death experience" to Elizabeth Kübler-Ross, renowned psychiatrist, author, and MD. I would be remiss if I did not include some more of her work here.

Elizabeth spent a large part of her lifetime consoling the grief-stricken. In the last book written before her death, she chided science as it tries to explain NDEs and their associated phenomena. Modern medicine and science try to explain them away, she wrote, "calling them hallucinations brought on by pain medication, or wishful thinking."[128]

She elaborated: "The dying experience is similar to that of birth, just as the growth of the caterpillar is the natural step toward emergence of the butterfly. Just as we cannot hear a dog whistle, which sounds at a frequency too high for the human ear, we cannot hear our loved one broadcasting on a channel whose frequency is beyond our ears' capabilities. But that doesn't mean our loved one can't hear us. A ship exists on the ocean, even if it sails out beyond the limits of our sight. The people in the ship have not vanished; they are simply moving to another shore.

"In the same way, death can be viewed as a transition to a higher state of consciousness where you continue to perceive, understand, and grow. The only thing you lose is something that you don't need any more, your physical body. It's like putting away your winter coat when spring arrives. You lose something that you don't need any more, something that may have been sick, old, and no longer in working order. That understanding may leave little comfort in the immediate moment, but in the long run, it helps to know that somewhere, somehow, our loved one still exists, and we will see them again."[129]

A few pages earlier she penned: "Birth is not a beginning and death is not an ending. They are merely points on a continuum. ..we believe with all our hearts that even in death, our loved one still exists. Life continues beyond the death of a physical body. It is only the warmth and calm of a transformation of a cocoon to a butterfly. You don't see the butterfly, but you feel the relief of knowing that your loved one is no longer in pain, no longer hooked up to tubes and sick in a bed; they are no longer diseased. Your loved one is now free of all that."[130]

When she was young, Kübler-Ross clearly recalled her visit to a concentration camp, where she couldn't help but notice the multitude of drawings of butterflies on the walls of the barracks. "I thought of all the places in the world where you might find butterflies, but never in a death camp. For the next twenty-five years, I wondered why there were so many butterflies, and now I know that the butterfly is a symbol of transformation, not of death, but of life continuing no matter what."[131]

Marisa St. Clair noted in her writings that Kübler-Ross was an atheist in her initial work with dying patients, but her convictions soon turned to that of an agnostic. Quoting Kübler-Ross, St. Clair wrote: "Even the angriest and most difficult patients very shortly before death began to deeply relax, have a sense of serenity around them, and were pain free in spite of perhaps a cancer-ridden body full of metastases. Also, the moment after death occurred, their facial features expressed an incredible sense of peace and equanimity and serenity which I could not comprehend since it was often a death that occurred in a state of anger, bargaining or depression."

In scanning all the books I have read and consulted in writing this book, I am somewhat amazed at the number of scientists and medical doctors who have experienced NDEs. In his work entitled *Light and Death*, Dr. Michael Salom wrote: "It used to be thought that the point of death was a single moment in time. But it is now thought that death is a process, not a single moment."[132] His thoughts similarly reflect those of Kübler-Ross.

Paralleling Kübler-Ross's comments about scientists being doubtful of paranormal phenomena and NDEs, Higgins wrote: "Many mainstream scientists are skeptics...because they are wary of anything that cannot be measured or quantified. The very same scientists, who are pretty closed-minded when it comes to accepting paranormal phenomena, talk of black holes and dark matter without batting an eyelid, even though there is no visible proof yet that they exist. They will dismiss without a thought the theories of supernatural and the paranormal while at the same time propounding contradictory theories with extraordinary claims."[133]

I discovered one big skeptic named Michael Newton in my research for this book. He labels himself as a skeptic by nature. His occupations include counseling and psychotherapy. However, over ten years, he collected many stories from his clients, who, under hypnosis, related their NDEs to him. "I am not a religious person, but I have found where we go after death to be one of order and direction, and I have come to appreciate that there is a grand design to life and afterlife."[134]

Newton admits early on in his book that he is/was an atheist. He found that his clients did not remember their experiences of "temporary death" or NDEs, but people in a *deep* trance state were able to describe what life is like after permanent physical death. He explained, "If death were the end of everything about us, then life indeed would be meaningless."[135]

Newton also found that it was "possible to see into the spirit world through the mind's eye of a hypnotized subject who could report back to me of life between lives on Earth."[136] In detailing 29 case studies, he described how it feels to die, what you see and feel right after death, spiritual guides, among other topics that are familiar to others who have studied the phenomenon of NDEs.

French physician Jean Jacques Charbonier collected evidence from several hundred patients who gave accounts of returning from clinical death. He found that at least 60 million have had such an experience following cardiac arrest. In his 25 years of practicing intensive care medicine, Charbonier, like Kübler-Ross, Salom, and others, suggested that death is a transition, rather than an end. He supported seven good reasons to believe in the afterlife, which you, as the reader, can find thoroughly covered in his book.

I found it interesting that in the Foreword to Charbonier's book, another French doctor, Oliver Chambon, wrote: "Only that which is essential—our consciousness, our knowledge, our capacity to love, and our loving connections—is carried over into the hereafter."[137] He also mentioned Professor Kenneth Ring, who claimed that the long-term positive impact of NDE on the life of those who have been through one can be practically transmitted, like a sort of positive virus, to those who read the accounts of these "experiences."

Investigative journalist Patricia Pearson spent a lot of time writing about Bruce Greyson's contributions to NDE studies. Greyson developed the Near-Death Experience Scale, which includes sixteen items. Any NDE that scored seven out of sixteen is termed a *classic NDE*--the greater the number of items, the more profound the NDE. Near-death researchers Robert and Suzanne Mays place Dr. Eben Alexander's NDE, for example, as scoring very high on the Greyson NDE Scale. They firmly believe his experience "was a genuine NDE."[138]

Here are some of those terms included in the Scale: undergoing a life review; experiencing cosmic unity; receiving new knowledge or insight; feelings of peace; seeming to enter another landscape or world; being surrounded by light; encountering other beings; and undergoing a life review. Greyson states that "mental clarity, vivid sensory imagery, a memory of the experience, and a conviction that the experience seemed 'more real than real'"[139] are the most commonly found norms. He also found that 56 percent of Westerners who have NDEs experience themselves going out of body. He continues:

"People remember the emotional content of the NDE with extreme clarity, regardless of its symbolic or cultural content."[140]

Greyson asked people to describe their NDEs years later, and he found no differences from the way they described the experiences the first time. In using the Memory Characteristics Questionnaire (MCQ), he discovered their memories were *more real* than real events, just as real events were remembered as more real than imagined events. "Their memories of the NDE had more detail, more clarity, more context, and more intense feelings than memories of real events."[141] Two other studies, in Italy and Belgium, found the same results. Indeed, the Belgian researchers found that those who had NDEs had profoundly sharp memories of the experience, which were filled with unique, clear, and sharp details. Thonnard et al.'s study also determined that "NDEs cannot be considered as imagined events."[142] Greyson and these other researchers remarked how these intense memories were never "confabulated" over time, with the passage of time never materially distorting the NDE memories at all.

Another Belgian study conducted by neurologist Steven Laureys suggested that what makes NDEs "unique" is not being "near-death" but rather the *perception* of the NDE itself.[143] But, as Pearson notes, NDEs take place while the brain should not have "any kind of coherent thought process at all, regardless of whether you want to call that process a dream, a memory, or an elaborate hallucination. Science has yet to explain how that could be. Severe brain impairment due to oxygen deprivation or powerful sedation doesn't set up the right conditions for incisive thought." She concludes, "What is striking about NDEs is how the thread of consciousness continues, featuring a coherent sequence of thoughts, from the person being awake to finding themselves in an altered state."[144]

Two questions posed by Greyson included: "Might it be possible that our minds could continue to function after our brains have stopped permanently—that is, after we die?" and "If our consciousness doesn't end when our bodies die, then where does it go?"[145] Good questions!

Greyson theorizes: "If the mind were in fact produced by electrical and chemical changes in the brain, then near-death experiences that happen when the brain is not functioning should be impossible. If the mind is completely dependent on the brain, how could you have a NDE? How could you have vivid and even heightened feelings, thinking, and memory formation when your heart has stopped, and your brain activity is largely gone?

"NDEs during cardiac arrest and deep anesthesia, when the brain is not able to process experiences and form memories, led me to seek some alternative to the idea that 'the mind is what the brain does!' Again, the furniture in my worldview was starting to fall over. If the brain is not the source of all our thoughts and feelings, then how *do* we explain what's going on with NDEs?"[146] More good questions!

C.C. French (2005) noted that during the minutes that pass between cardiac arrest and the death of the brain stem, the patient's mind experiences "vivid and varied images. It seems that these lead into a final experience that totally resolves all personal conflicts, all unanswered questions, all emotional loose ends, all guilt, remorse and sorrow, as the consciousness enters a state of warmth, joy and release from pain, characterized by NDEers as being overwhelmingly suffused with love. In a word, it is transformative."[147]

Roger Cook described this transformation of consciousness as a conundrum: *"Nothing leaves the body at death, yet we do experience a personal heaven. The experience occupies only a moment of time, yet creates an eternity in death, at which point the dimension of time is extinguished."*[148] He added: "The foregoing is an organic perspective on the near-death evidence, firmly grounded in the idea that everything humans experience at death is a product of the brain."[149]

On the cover of Pearson's book, Larry Dorsey, MD, commented, "You don't die when you die. That's the message from around fifteen million Americans who have experienced a near-death experience." The number is not the issue; it is the commonality of these very numerous conditions, especially since our advances in medicine strive to keep people alive as long as possible (since doctors do all they can to maintain the standards they are sworn to uphold in the Hippocratic Oath).

Psychiatrist Bruce Greyson studied NDEs over a span of four decades. He noted early on in his work that he was raised with no religious belief system whatsoever, so he was not predisposed into believing in any religious or spiritual background that could slant or bias his study. He openly admitted: "People from different cultures and different religions have NDEs, *whether or not they believe in them.* Some of the experiences…describe things that contradict their cultural and religious beliefs. Some were atheists who didn't believe in a higher power or in anything after death—but who can't deny their experience of somehow being conscious when their bodies were declared dead. It seems clear to me that the study of near-death experiences can be a rigorous, empirical, observational science."[150]

Pearson offered solid evidence that people in indigenous cultures never reported going through a tunnel. Instead, they passed through some other types of landscapes that their culture was familiar with. She stated, "Perhaps we encounter what we can emotionally and conceptually relate to. People remember the emotional context of the NDE with extreme clarity, regardless of its symbolic or cultural content."[151]

I have provided my readers with quite an extensive exposure to all the research that has been done on NDEs to display the inexplicable. Yet another researcher must be added to my list. He is Kevin Nelson, a neurologist who collected data from 55 patients. In his data, he noticed how life experience, cultural background, and individual and shared biology shaped NDEs.

Nelson is particularly interested in brain studies, as evidenced in this quote: "The brain is nowhere near physically dead during NDEs. It is alive and conscious."[152] He was also intrigued with Van Lommel's studies, in which 344 consecutive patients who were resuscitated from cardiac arrest exhibited no EEG readings. In other words, they were clinically dead.

However, only 62 of these 344 experienced NDEs. Nelson thoroughly detailed how brain death occurs with the death of cells that burst like a balloon when it is punctured by a pin. Such action in the brain is due to a lack of blood. Brain cells cannot re-grow or regenerate. Permanent brain damage should occur 30 minutes after blood flow to the brain is reduced by 90 percent or more.

He retells Dr. Sanjay Gupta's account of a person in Norway who fell into a cold stream and was trapped under ice for 90 minutes. A helicopter transported her blue, lifeless body to the nearest hospital after a flight time of more than one hour. Her body temperature was 58 degrees, and her heart did not beat for hours. She did fully recover, and she now is working as a radiologist! Her brain never died, since the freezing water placed her neurons into suspended animation, so her brain cells would not burst like balloons.

Nelson ends his book by suggesting that we all view the brain as a spiritual organ. He says that believing in experiences outside the brain (and outside our medical and scientific explanation) is faith. "It's folly to expect that science can prove or disprove the truthfulness of these experiences. The nature of faith makes it immune to science's demands for consensus, verification, and prediction."[153] Nelson warns that in answering the question "What does it mean to have a spiritual brain?" mankind does not make a "Faustian deal with the devil, potentially transforming us from god to God. We would have the potential to provoke events such as Jonestown many times over."[154]

Returning to Dr. Jeffrey Long, who was discussed earlier in this chapter, I learned that he compiled over 4,000 NDE reports into a list of the most common reflections offered by his patients:

- Leaving my body confirmed to me that we can exist outside of the physical body.
- We live on—eternally. There is no death. Simply a passing or a return to home.
- There was an awareness that there is life after physical/earthly death.
- I was aware that I was somewhere that was magnificent and where I was surrounded with people I knew were dead—I was filled with love and felt loved.[155]

From his extended study, he reached a dramatic conclusion: "Medically speaking, near-death experiences should be impossible."[156] Just like Pearson, Greyson, and others, the striking element of NDEs, Long found, is the fact that "the thread of consciousness continues, featuring a coherent sequence of thoughts, from the person being awake to finding themselves in an altered state. This is not what happens when we slip from wakefulness into dreams."[157]

Pearson noted that "in the aftermath of their NDEs, people describe the world around them as flat, dull, two-dimensional, filled with stick figures and 'paper cutout dolls.' Asked simple 'agree' or 'disagree' questions, 56 percent agree that the NDE realms were '1,000 times stronger' as a reality than their everyday reality."[158]

She also detailed the near-death experience of Carl Jung, one of the most well-known psychologists, in his own words: "The view of the city and mountains from my sickbed seemed to me like a painted curtain with black holes in it, or a tattered sheet of newspaper full of photographs that meant nothing. Disappointed, I thought, 'Now I must return to the 'box system' again.' For it seemed to me as if behind the horizon of the cosmos a three-dimensional world had been artificially built up, in which each person sat by himself in a little box. And now I should have to convince myself all over again that this was important."

Researchers found that individual's NDEs reflected their perceptions that were founded by their own belief systems, based upon their own unique life experiences, spirituality, and religious symbolism. For instance, people who were, let's say, Chinese non-Christians, did not report seeing a Being of Light, but rather super-beautiful mountains, greenery, flowers, and gardens. Worldwide, Christian or not, about 50 percent of NDEers journeyed beyond encountering the Light and they perceived gardens of cities.[159]

In many local, state, national, and international conferences and seminars that I have attended over years and years in the educational realm, I have heard speakers proclaim: "Perception is reality until proven otherwise." If we apply that quote to NDEs, we can plainly see that the way(s) in which those who have experienced previews of the next life are truly based on their perceptions, inherent or otherwise. If those perceptions are based on faith and a lack of fear of death and dying and the "great beyond," which Christians believe is Heaven, who among scientists and medical personnel on Earth would dare to disprove the validity of those perceptions? Some have tried! But they have failed!

To discover "what is nonsense, and what is scientifically debunked," the Immortality Project was instituted with a $5 million grant by the John Templeton Foundation to philosopher John Fisher in 2012. Fisher stated, "People have been thinking about immortality throughout history. We have a deep human need to figure out what happens to us after death. No one has taken a comprehensive and sustained look at immortality that brings together the science, theology and philosophy. We will be very careful in documenting near-death experiences and other phenomena, trying to figure out if these offer plausible glimpses of an afterlife or are biologically induced illusions."[160]

Fisher's studies resulted in his co-authoring a book with Mitchell-Yellin, in which they claimed that our current technology is not capable of measuring all brain activity. They described the technology as "shallow" and that the possibility exists that patients who had NDEs had their brains functioning at levels that are "undetectable by our current methods."[161]

Another researcher in this Project, Andrew Eshelman, wrote, "I will seek to extend the view to language about an afterlife in which the kingdom of God is brought to fruition."[162]

In addition, psychologist Kurt Gray added this comment to the research collected by the Project: "Our research has also examined the emotional nature of dying, and had revealed that it may be less negative than we might think. We examined the language of death row last words and the blog posts of terminally ill patients, and revealed that its emotional content is actually more positive than people predict."[163]

# Quantum Consciousness, Biocentrism, and the Theory of a Natural Afterlife

I quoted cardiologist Dr. Sam Parnia earlier in this chapter when he noted how "consciousness continues even though the brain has completely shut down," and that he viewed this consciousness as having some type of physicality, a "subtle force; essentially quantum consciousness."[164]

But what exactly is this *quantum consciousness*? We have looked at a large amount of research, and I owe it to you, my readers, to tackle this research topic as well. Briefly, this theory holds that the second a person dies, quantum information is released from his or her microtubules into the universe. I will explain microtubules shortly.

Regardless, if the dying person is resuscitated, the quantum information (or we might call it the soul) is funneled back into the microtubules, causing a NDE. "If they're not revived, and the patient dies, it's possible that this quantum information can exist outside the body, perhaps indefinitely, as a soul," claim the two developers of this theory, Penrose and Hameroff.

Microtubules are found inside the brain. "They are tubular structures inside eukaryotic cells (part of the cytoskeleton) that play a role in determining the cell's shape, as well as its movements, which includes cell division—separation of chromosomes during mitosis."[165]

---

Those two developers are named Sir Roger Penrose, a physicist and Nobel Prize candidate, and Stuart Hameroff, professor and anesthesiologist. They labeled the process involving microtubules as "Orchestrated Objective Reduction" (Orch-OR). In this process, they claimed that protein-based microtubules, which are a structural element present in human cells, carry this quantum information, and store it at a sub-atomic level.[166] Hameroff added: "Let's say the heart stops beating, the blood stops flowing; the micro-tubules lose their quantum status.

"The quantum information within the micro-tubules is not destroyed. It can't be destroyed, and it just distributes and dissipates to the universe at large.

"If the patient is resuscitated, revived, this quantum information can go back, not the micro-tubules, and the patient says, 'I had a near-death experience.'"[167]

Dr. Hans-Peter Dunn, former head of the world-renowned Max Planck Institute for Physics, which is housed in Munich, stated: "What we consider the here and now, this world, it is actually just the material level that is comprehensible. The beyond is an infinite reality that is much bigger."[168]

The quantum theory "doesn't mean that upon death we are conscious of ourselves (or carry with us our personalities) but that our consciousness or memories will return to the universe, perhaps even feeding into a sort of cosmic library: the profundity of ourselves filtering back into its primordial truth."[169] To me, that "truth" means the Light!

In 2010, Hameroff and Deepak Chopra raised the following possibility: "Recently two clinical studies used processed EEG brain monitors at the time of death in terminally ill or severely brain-damaged patients from whom support was withdrawn, allowing the patients to die peacefully. In both sets of patients, measurable EEG brain activity dwindled as blood pressure dropped, and eventually the heart stopped beating. But then, in each patient, there was an abrupt burst of brain activity lasting about a minute or more which correlated with gamma synchrony EEG, the most reliable marker of conscious awareness. Then, just as abruptly, the activity ceased. Because the patients died, we can't know if they had NDE or OOB [out of body] experiences, or if the activity actually marked the soul leaving the body – 'giving up the ghost.' But regardless, the mystery is how the energy-depleted brain could muster synchronous neuronal EEG activity – whatever it was. One possible answer is that consciousness and gamma synchrony involve very low energy quantum entanglements, which persist while other brain functions have run out of fuel."[170]

One of the newest scientific theories, called biocentrism, was postulated by Robert Lanza, who asked, "Does the soul exist?" He claims that we are immortal beings who exist outside of time. So, when we are fully dead, we are alive without time, in eternity.

In his own words, Lanza states: "There are an infinite number of universes, and everything that could possibly happen occurs in some universe. Death does not exist in any real sense in these scenarios. All possible universes exist simultaneously, regardless of what happens in any of them. Although individual bodies are destined to self-destruct, the alive feeling—the 'Who am I?' – is just a 20-watt fountain of energy operating in the brain. But this energy doesn't go away at death. One of the surest axioms of science is that energy never dies; it can neither be created nor destroyed. But does this energy transcend from one world to another?"[171]

I believe that God, the Light, has the answer. He is the great I Am! He is the source of all energy, and He cannot be created. He is THE Creator!

He cannot be destroyed, since He is the ultimate source of life, light, and energy. But science always looks for a scientific analysis for its answers. Some of the researchers are looking at a spiritual answer that defies man's attempts to explain the incomprehensible, the unexplainable, until we all encounter the Light in eternity.

Another newer theory is that of a natural afterlife, proposed by Bryon Ehlmann. It can be stated as follows: "The natural afterlife of a NDE-enabled creature is the NDE from which it never awakes—essentially, a never-ending experience (NEE) relative to the creature's perception."[172] This approach distinguishes a NDE from an afterlife experience based on the perception of the individual involved. Ehlmann offers: "When the NDE ends in death, the dying person simply transitions from a dynamic into a static state of mind. The final moment of the NDE becomes the NEE."[173]

The theory maintains that only those around you when you are in a NDE realize that your NDE ended in death, but the person dying does not have this realization. Ehlmann continues: "What's peculiar about the natural afterlife and key to understanding it is this: it's not about realizing you're in the afterlife *after* you've died, as humans have always imagined, but about realizing you're there *before* you've died and then never knowing otherwise." The NDE and the NEE are relative, everlasting and timeless.

The theorist claims that you are in a "paused" conscious state during a NDE, while in the NEE, having lost all subsequent perception, you are in a forever present. He reminds the reader that when we fall asleep while watching a movie or lying in bed, we never perceive the moment that we entered such a state of unconsciousness. Similarly, if we pass out from a general anesthesia, or end a dream and awaken, "then it is extremely likely they never perceive the moment of death while unconscious and dying, with or without the NDE…the NEE theory is *nearly* proven by logical deduction."[174]

Surely, this theory cannot *yet* be verified, Ehlmann heralds, but it is "at least plausible." Based on the existing scientific explanations of NDEs, their reality and intensity, he sees this theory as superior to others that try to explain a *spiritual* natural afterlife. Citing the work of Zingrone and Alvarado (2009), Ehlmann writes: "When a heavenly NDE ends with death and events have ceased, likely the most important part that remains in the NEE are the heightened emotions—often love, joy, and peace. *And they are real!*" Thus, these emotions travel with the person into the afterlife.

What I found to be extremely interesting was the content of Ehlmann's Appendix. In vivid detail, he likens the natural afterlife to being in a state of permanent general anesthesia! He mentions Hameroff, the famous anesthesiologist: "It's still incredible that they're awake, they go to sleep, and come back the same person. Where do they go? We can learn a lot about consciousness from anesthesia."

Moreover, Ehlmann pursues this analogy with listing how the natural afterlife is like permanent general anesthesia in seven ways, yet different from it in only three ways. Without all the hoopla and formulas attached in the Appendix, suffice it to say that "the lack of dreaming (which is not true with sleeping) makes the permanent anesthesia analogy excellent for understanding the concept of a timeless, forever moment."

The seven ways in which the natural afterlife is *like* being permanently anesthetized include:

1. Your last perceived moment includes an anticipation of more such moments to come. When saying "92" in counting backwards from 100 on the operating table, you fully anticipate within that moment to next be saying "91" in the same room to the same people—even despite knowing that your experience here will soon end in an unconscious state (which you will not know in an NDE). However, unknowingly, you never say "91."

2. Your mind never gets the message that "you've passed out" (more precisely "passed away" with the natural afterlife). Instead, you merely lose your sense of time.

3. You never lose your sense of self. You remain "the same person," never having to ask "Who am I?" (same with dreaming and dreamless sleep).

4. You won't experience nothingness; the concept is meaningless. Hameroff states that patients under general anesthesia experience no passage of time.

Thus both are timeless and there is simply no time to experience nothingness.

5. You won't dream. Hameroff states that patients don't dream under general anesthesia (making it an internal state…Such dreams would create another moment of time replacing the moment last experienced on the operating table, likewise with the natural afterlife last experienced in the NDE.

6. Your memory, whether taken offline by anesthesia or wiped out by death, is useless and anyway superfluous. Memory fragments need not be assessed since you're dreaming and besides, timelessness makes such access purposeless.

7. Your last perceived moment, on the operating table, or in your NDE, is timeless and everlasting since you never wake up.

In contrast, the three ways in which the natural afterlife is *unlike* being permanently anesthetized are as follows:

1. Your NDE is not like the tedium of counting backwards from 100 while people hover over you. Rather, NDEs are often described as more intense than a party drug hallucination and seem to pack a wallop on the people experiencing them, often having a tremendous impact on the rest of their lives. So, the last moment of the NDE surely provides a much sharper "imprint on the mind" than does the last moment of counting backwards.

2. In your NDE you may firmly believe that "I've arrived" and my future is here. Not so in counting backwards from 100 and believing this monotony will be short-lived.

3. With an imperceptible death, you likely feel no grogginess, the going in and out of consciousness, as you may experience in passing out under anesthesia. (You also feel no grogginess in transitioning from dreaming into dreamless sleep.) Thus, there's no hint whatsoever that your NDE is over—which again, relatively speaking, makes your natural afterlife everlasting.[175]

**So, after all this research, do scientists and medical personnel have a solid explanation for NDEs?**

If Dr. Moody were to answer this question, he would tell the "armchair investigators," as he calls them, to back off. The original researcher of NDEs, Moody has seen it all and read it all. My work only touches the surface. His does not. Many other researchers have developed hypotheses and theories to answer this question. BUT, the final answer rests in the Hands of God.

We curious humans still search for the elusive answer, which is admirable. Moody and others chastise the journalists and "armchair investigators" who attempt to have a definitive answer or critique. Moody remarks, for example, on those who criticize one of his colleagues, Dr. Alexander: "Most, if not all of them, have never actually interviewed people who have undergone these profound experiences. Instead, these armchair investigators offer only ungrounded speculation about the cause or origins of such experiences based on their analytical assessment of the findings published by other researchers who do the actual field work. But actual interviews with people who report near-death experiences leave one with quite a different impression."[176]

Indeed, Eben Alexander, a renowned professor of neurosurgery at Harvard Medical School, has faced a lot of criticism. Moody writes in his book review of Alexander's NDE: "Dr.Eben Alexander's near-death experience stands as perhaps one of the crown jewels of all near-death experiences. The knowledge of what he experienced raises the bar for serious investigators and pundits…thanks to his great courage in laying his superb credentials and reputation on the line by coming forward with his story."[177]

In summary, if we asked Dr. Alexander to tell us what he learned from his NDE, here is his answer:

1. We are each eternal beings – our essence is eternal – we are temporarily wearing this "costume" (our physical body) in this "act of the play." When the act is over, we doff our costume and reunite with our "higher soul" which has always known the truth and purpose of our existence.

2. The single most important force or principle in the Universe is unconditional Love – It is at the core of all existence, as the unconditional love of the Creator of all of Creation – It provides the infinite energy for healing self, others and the whole world.

3. We are all One, all joined energetically, manifestations of Om – One Consciousness, or Creative Essence, gives rise to our sense of individual consciousness - the apparent boundaries between individuals are all illusory, emergent property, and these ultimately give rise to our notion of "self" and "ego" existing in this realm, along with all of our perceptions of "physical reality."

4. That Creative essence IS our conscious awareness – the spark of Divinity within us all, temporarily/partially

veiled from our incarnations, so that we can judge ourselves on our proper decisions based on free will when reconnected with our higher souls.

5. This truth is cleverly veiled from us to enable our souls to manifest expressions of that unconditional love from the Creator based on faith and belief, even in the face of all the moral evil and injustice so rampant in this imperfect physical realm.

6. The purpose of all existence is to allow our souls' manifestation of free will – Love serves as the perfect moral compass in all decisions made in this imperfect physical realm – offering our ascendance in the Spiritual Realm, by manifesting that love of the Creator to all fellow beings.

7. The Creator is behind the numbers, the perfection of the universe that science measures and struggles to understand. But – perhaps paradoxically – the Creator is also every bit as "human" as you and I are, understanding and sympathizing with our human nature more profoundly and personally than we (as humans in this physical plane) can imagine.

8. All together, we form all aspects of the Creator – becoming Oneness. During our passage through the physical (dualist) realm, forcing half-truths to be absolute truths is the cause for much angst. Absolute truths exist only in the spiritual (non-dualist) realm, yet our ascendance as souls is towards the Oneness, the acknowledgement that all of our existence is the one Consciousness. Experiencing a sense of self and of the Oneness simultaneously is the "new duality."

9. Hardship and difficulties in life are opportunities for our spiritual growth here in "soul school."

10. Our souls "travel in packs" helping each other to set up and learn the lessons necessary for our progression in the Spiritual realm, i.e. in choosing these lives.
11. Some of our soul partners may manifest as what appears to be our nemesis in this incarnation, helping us learn certain lessons.[178]

I have spent a good portion of my academic life learning, teaching, and researching the world of journalism. Soon after I had earned my Doctorate in Education, I was dubbed Dr. Joe Positive. I have worked hard to maintain a positive attitude about life, at least most of the time. That was not always true. But I know in my heart, mind, and soul that I am a changed individual. That "fact" was made clear by the Light that manages all, the Great Power in Heaven. Of what do I speak?

At the foot of The Cross in Groom, Texas, on May 30, 2008, I was born again in Spirit; I had a heart-to-heart conversation with God. I left there knowing I was a changed individual, a born-again Christian. I don't care whether you believe me, or not! I know it to be true.

I also know that I had experienced a NDE earlier in my life. I recall the details just as if it had happened yesterday. Each time I relate the experience to someone, it never changes. Such is the substance of truth. If you do not lie, the story's details do not change.

Unfortunately, I see very little "true" journalism taking place in the world today. I have grown to detest "fake news" and all it stands for. Whatever happened to telling the viewers the truth simply by answering the basic questions every true journalist should tell his or her viewers: Who? What? When? Where?

Why? How? These are called the 5 W's and 1 H. This is taught in Journalism 101.

Inserting one's own biased/slanted opinion has no place in the world of journalism, unless both sides of the topic are presented. However, that rarely takes place in today's media, whether in print, broadcast, or Internet formats. The result? Negativity and misinformation.

The same is true of the topic of NDEs. Some journalists, who call themselves investigative reporters, insert just a bit too much of their own opinions and biases in their stories. These are the "armchair investigators," as Moody termed them. One such writer in the case of Dr. Alexander's NDE is Luke Dittrich of *Esquire* magazine.

In the August 2013 issue of Esquire, Dittrich shed a huge shadow of doubt on the truth, the credibility, of Alexander's experience. Yes, he did spend a considerable amount of time interviewing the Doctor, but Dittrich is not the Doctor, and he had never experienced a NDE himself. The multi-page feature article is too lengthy to dissect and analyze precisely point-by-point. So let me condense its message here.

*Proof of Heaven* was not the title that Alexander selected for his book. It was suggested by an ABC executive in a meeting with Alexander's publisher. Dittrich admits, "In his study, toward the end of our conversation, Alexander distances himself from the title.

'When they first came to me with that title I didn't like it at all. Because I knew from my journey that it was very clear to me that no human brain or mind, no kind of scientific philosophical entity will ever be able to know enough to say yes or no to the existence of that realm or deity, because it's so far beyond human understanding.

'It is, he says, "laughable" and "the highest form of folly, of hubris" to think that anyone could ever "prove" heaven. I knew, he says, that proof in a scientific sense was ridiculous. I mean, no one could have that.'[179]

Throughout the expose, the writer concentrates on three flaws in Alexander's story: the heralding rainbow that could not have been witnessed; the shout for help that could not have been uttered; and, the hyper-real experience that could not have occurred in a medically induced coma. Dissecting a coma, the Dalai Lama pronounced Eben Alexander unreliable and a liar. The characteristics of a genuine near-death experience, a corroborating time anchor, and a "Peak in Darien" experience are discussed as a further confirmation of the alleged falsehood of Alexander's account. If you are interested in pursuing your own in-depth reading, please consult the Reference information located at the end of this book.

If, however, you desire an abridged version, be sure to read an article in the References section of this book, that of Robert and Suzanne Mays, who are authentic near-death researchers. They are not journalists, "armchair investigators," or doctors. Their conclusion, after a very thorough analysis of the *Esquire* article, is "The content of Luke Dittrich's article certainly raises the question as to what standards were applied to it by *Esquire*. In my opinion, Mr. Dittrich's actions investigating and writing the article and *Esquire*'s unabashed endorsement of it rise to the level of malpractice."[180]

Should you read the *Esquire* article itself, you will note the lengthy amount of print devoted to listing several malpractice accusations leveled against Dr. Alexander, as well as any settlements on those accusations or claims. Mays added: "Malpractice is not ordinarily used for journalistic practice. However, there are certain informal ethics and standards of behavior that apply, particularly within a given publishing organization."[181]

Mays accused the magazine of labeling Alexander a complete fraud in the article; the facts were "distorted or completely wrong and the conclusions are totally unwarranted. And the result has been devastating to those people who know the facts and how utterly wrong they were portrayed in the article."[182]

What was Dr. Alexander's reaction? "I wrote a truthful account of my experiences in *Proof of Heaven* and have acknowledged in the book both my professional and personal accomplishments and my setbacks. I stand by every word in this book and have made its message the purpose of my life. *Esquire*'s cynical article distorts the facts of my 25-year career as a neurosurgeon and is a textbook example of how unsupported assertions and cherry-picked information can be assembled at the expense of truth."[183]

**So, after all the research, theories, and exploration, is science any closer to a solid explanation for NDEs, consciousness, and life after death?**

Since our first habitation on this earth, man has been curious about the world around him. That curiosity extended into the world in which he had no knowledge, in which he had no physicality, or at least that is what he/she thought! But mankind has always wondered: what awaits us after we die? Therefore, it should be no wonder that we still are grappling with this question.

George Nixon suggests: "We, however, are the only animals that know *conceptually* of our inevitable demise, yet despite our mortal knowledge we have devised brilliant or insane means of avoiding the truth. **Death is good.** It is not the opposite of life but the necessary polarity of life: it is part of the life cycle and most entities in Nature simply live their cycles until those cycles cease to repeat. Nature does not question and Nature does not regret. Life goes on.

"It seems certain to me that **I** will die and stay dead. By 'I', I mean me, Greg Nixon, this person, this identity. I am so intertwined with the chiasmus of lives, bodies, ecosystems, symbolic intersubjectivity, and life on this particular planet that I cannot imagine this identity continuing alone without them.

"However, I can imagine, and often do, that there is a core consciousness, an inner light, a soul if you wish, that has always been with me, that lies as deeply within my being as the farthest star without. Perhaps this inner *essence* can continue on as light energy or some such thing without my personal identity – but not necessarily without any of my memories."[184]

It seems that Nixon's views reflect mine: that our memories, all that makes us unique individuals, our consciousness, follow us into the next realm. Other doctors, researchers, and scientists mentioned in this book would agree. Our souls, our inner lights (which are connected to the Source of all Light, *The* Light), survive death.

This leads to another question: Is this afterlife, this realm, a fourth dimension in which we have always lived, but are not aware of it until we shed our physical bodies in this world of three dimensions?

Dr. Stankovich believed it is so. Limited by "our sensorial perceptions," he asked us to "...imagine that we not only exist in the fourth dimension, but also that we will continue existing in the fourth dimension, after we disappear from the third."[185] Perhaps a sensitivity and awareness of this fourth dimension is a gift that true mediums and psychics are tuned into? Wouldn't this dimension-sensitivity explain some of the mystery surrounding the entire question: After we die, then what? Do those who have NDEs enter this fourth dimension and then return to the third? Hmmm!

Interestingly enough, Stankovich thoroughly described his theory by summarizing the bases of hypotheses that support the existence of a fourth dimension. For your thoughtful consideration, I will duplicate those for you right now:

1. The fourth dimension is logically consistent with the three dimensions accessible to our sensorial perception.
2. Time and space in the fourth dimension are different from those in the third, although they are in a way linked to the phenomena of the latter.
3. In the fourth dimension, there is a type of energy we do not know in the third ($E = MC^2$). The form of energy we know is a variation of that existing in the fourth dimension. Or, rather, the opposite.
4. The fourth dimension coexists simultaneously with the third, like this latter coexists simultaneously with the first two.

5. We cannot perceive the fourth dimension with our senses.
6. We do not know how one can pass from the third dimension to the fourth. However, we seek this step by intuition before being able to calculate it mathematically.
7. Some phenomena that are inexplicable in the third dimension are probably influenced by the effects of the fourth dimension.

Due to the differences between the third and fourth dimension, we can assume that the effects of the physical death of a human being in the third dimension are not the same in the fourth dimension, especially because of the characteristics of a person's psychic life. The most important consequences deduced from the above are the hypotheses that:

A. After physical death of a person in the third dimension, his/her existence in the fourth dimension can, somehow, continue.
B. Person's psychic existence, linked to biophysical factors in terms of energy, no longer receives this energy, but does receive the one that has always existed in the fourth dimension.
C. Therefore, even though the human being can continue indefinitely in the fourth dimension, he/she cannot go back to the third.
D. Physically, an individual who stops existing in the third dimension continues to exist in the fourth, at the same level he/she had in the third.

Epistemologically, the degree of certainty of the aforementioned seven points, as a whole, is greater than that of the four hypotheses deduced. The four hypotheses deduced are not yet scientific, because they still have to be proved, but their proof is already close to scientific examination.[186]

Thereafter, Stankovich explained what he termed *anthropoligion* or human religion. Of course, he stated that human religion is not based on science. But he claimed that it does assume the existence of the fourth dimension. "It is not based on any kind of revelation, but on the hypotheses that encompass the fundamental part of conventional religious topics people have been familiar with over thousands of years.

"It is commonly thought on a scientific level that religions were created because the primitive man could not find explanations for many natural phenomena due to his ignorance. So he attributed them to supernatural forces, which later gave way to religious beliefs.

"This anthropological hypothesis is quite plausible, but if the existence of the fourth dimension is proven, it could mean that the very early appearance of ideas about afterlife, beside the anthropological explanation, might have come from an obscure intuition of the possible prolongation of human life in the fourth dimension.

"The earthly human life is, in a way, preparation for the life in the fourth dimension. The life of an individual in the fourth dimension depends on what he or she does in this world, because each individual remains at the same level of possibilities he or she has created during his/her existence on Earth."[187]

It has often been said by medical personnel present at the scene of grave injury and possible death of a patient that the sense of hearing is the last sense to leave the physical body. Hence, Emergency Medical Personnel responding to a call are taught to speak to a person needing their help. So, in essence, if this is true, what happens to our other senses, our "sensorial perceptions," as Stankovich called them?

In their administration and study of the MCQ (Johnson et al.. {1988}), researchers discovered that NDEers did not accurately describe their memories of "sounds, smells, and tastes the event" probably because "they were not in their physical bodies at the time" and that their NDE "did not take place in a familiar physical environment, rendering sensory details less relevant." [188] All other factors measured by the MCQ were considerably greater than those dealing with the sensory details of the NDE.

Cardiologist Michael Sabom looked at temporal lobe or psychical seizures as a way to explain NDEs. But he found those different from NDEs in several ways. There is no "distorted perception of the immediate environment, emotions of fear, sadness, and loneliness, senses of smell and taste are present, only a single past event is involved and forced thinking is present...these definitely differ in NDEs."[189] But some NDEers claim that they DO have a sense of sight, smell, sound, and taste in their journey to the Other Side!

One such person is Rhoda "Jubilee" Mitchell, who tells about her sensory impressions of her NDE in the book *Heaven is Beyond Your Wildest Expectations: Ten True Stories of Experiencing Heaven.* She describes the songs being sung in

Heaven "like the song of a siren, captivating to the soul. The songs were so beautiful that no one wanted to miss a word or a note being sung. I am still curious about how the singers sang as high as they did. They hit notes that reached octaves above the highest pitches sung on earth. I enjoyed the diversity of the heavenly choirs. Some choirs were comprised of angels only. Some were mixed with humans, angels, and other creatures all praising and adoring God. The sights and sounds of the celestial city were magnificent!"

Where many others claimed to enter a tunnel and see a Light at its end, Mitchell witnessed "crowns on saints' heads (which) actually looked like thousands of points of light. To my amazement, the stars in the crowns were bits of real stars like the stars in the sky. It was a dazzling display when the saints turned to the left and right displaying their crowns, and shafts of light shone from each pinpoint of star. I have never seen anything on earth equal to it!"[190]

Some of the latest studies (2019) have compared, *linguistically*, the recollections of NDEers and those who took drugs, in particular ketamine. "This new study compared the stories of 625 individuals who reported NDEs with the stories of more than 15,000 individuals who had taken one of 165 psychoactive drugs. When those stories were linguistically analyzed, similarities were found between recollections of near-death and drug experiences for those who had taken a specific class of drug...ketamine led to experiences very similar to NDE. This may mean that the near-death experience may reflect changes in the same chemical system in the brain that is targeted by drugs like ketamine."[191]

All stories in this study were broken down into individual words, and the words were counted and sorted according to meanings. "The word most strongly represented in descriptions of both NDEs and ketamine experiences was 'reality,' highlighting the sense of presence that accompanies NDEs. High among the list of words common to both experiences were those related to perception (sight, color, voice, vision), the body (face, arm, foot), emotion (fear) and transcendence (universe, understand, consciousness).

"The famous hallucinogen LSD was as similar as ketamine to NDEs when the near-death event was caused by cardiac arrest." Admittedly, the researcher stated that "this study …is based on purely subjective reports."[192]

Finally, it proposed more research and more practical applications of its hypothesis. For example, it held that "because near-death experiences (NDEs) can be transformational and have profound and lasting effects on those who experience them, including a sense of fearlessness about death, the authors propose that ketamine could be used therapeutically to induce an NDE-like state in terminally ill patients as a 'preview' of what they might experience, so as to relieve their anxieties about death. That knowledge may ultimately contribute more to alleviating fear of this inevitable transition than a dose of any drug."[193]

Bruce Greyson and two colleagues, Emily Williams and Ian Stevenson, deeply probed the survival of consciousness after the death of the physical body. They concluded consciousness may function outside the physical body and thereby may survive physical death. "We emphasize that such evidence is only suggestive. No matter how serious their condition, persons reporting NDEs were in fact still alive in some sense, since their bodies were still functioning sufficiently to be revived. NDEs therefore never provide conclusive evidence concerning what may happen to consciousness when the brain and body are no longer revivable."[194]

Weighing all the research, particularly in science and physics, Dinesh D'Souza offered the following observations in his work, *Life after Death: The Evidence*: "…there is nothing in physics to contradict life after death. Unlike material objects and all other living creatures, we humans inhabit two domains: the way things are, and the way things ought to be (facts and values). Yet these values defy natural and scientific explanation because physical laws, as discovered by science, concern only the way things are and not the way they ought to be.

"Paradoxically, it is the world beyond the world that has made the greatest difference in our world. This means that life after death is not merely a rational and even probable belief; it is also a conviction that sustains and strengthens our civilization. The implication is that whatever happens to our bodies and brains after death, our souls live on."[195] The soul is that part of us that might outlast our mortal bodies. Furthermore, he concludes that free will and consciousness are the defining features of human souls, and that they operate outside of physical and scientific laws.

## Chapter IV

## What is That Light Seen by Many NDEers?

Gospel writer Matthew recorded a conversation that Jesus Christ once had with his followers regarding fear, as in any type of fear, even fear of death: "Whatever I tell you in the dark, speak in the light; and what you hear in the ear, preach on the housetops. And do not fear those who kill the body but cannot kill the soul. But rather fear Him who can destroy both soul and body in hell. Are not two sparrows sold for a copper coin? And not one of them falls to the ground apart from your Father's will. But the very hairs of your head are all numbered. Do not fear therefore; you are of more value than many sparrows."
--Matthew10:27-31

Are we of more value than sparrows because we have a soul, a life energy that follows us out of our physical body, but remains alive in the next life, one of eternal return to the source of our energy in the spiritual world? NDEers say YES! Energy can be transferred, not destroyed. Explain the photographic images that have been recorded with infrared film, of souls, spirits, lifting from operating tables as a patient is declared clinically dead. Explain how and why those declared dead and having experienced near-death events see their own spirits abandon their bodies only to return "for some reason."

Science and medicine, as we have seen, cannot fully explain NDEs. But faith can. Jesus Himself said, "I am the light of the world. He who follows Me shall not walk in darkness but have the light of life." --John 8:12

He also said, "I have come as a light into the world, that whoever believes in Me should not abide in darkness."
--John 12:46

1 John 1:5 states: "God is light, and in Him is no darkness at all." Indeed, in predicting His own death on the Cross, Christ, the Son of God, told his followers: "A little while longer the light is with you. Walk while you have the light, lest darkness overtake you; he who walks in darkness does not know where he is going." --John 12:36.

NDEers tell us they know where they went after "death." Most of them see the Light at the end of the Tunnel, and they describe the Spiritual Being as brighter than any light they have ever seen before on earth. Since the NDE experience is universal and we are told not to fear death by Jesus Himself, can science or medicine explain why even atheists and those who have never heard of the Bible, God, or Jesus, have similar visual experiences when they "die"?

Admitting that he once *was* an atheist, C.S. Lewis remarks: "When Christianity says that God loves man, it means that God *loves* man; not that He has some 'disinterested', because really indifferent, concern for our welfare, but that, in awful and surprising truth, we are the objects of His love. You asked for a loving God; you have one. How this should be, I do not know; it passes reason to explain why any creatures, not to say creatures such as we, should have a value so prodigious in their Creator's eyes."[196] As a lover of famous quotations, I would like to add what C.S. Lewis stated after becoming a Christian: "I gave in and admitted that God was God."

Let me digress for a short time and enter a "Time Machine." In the early days of the COVID-19 pandemic in 2020, I ended up teaching online with my students at the Shepherd School of Language in Las Vegas. One of the topics we discussed was Ayn

Rand's book *Anthem*, akin to George Orwell's *1984*. How does Rand relate to my book that you are currently reading?

Well, in 1947, an essayist named B. Royce penned an analysis of the famous Russian composer Tchaikovsky's religious beliefs, and published it on Rand's forum designed for her fans. Entitled *Russian Symphony: Thoughts about Tchaikovsky*, Royce related how Tchaikovsky wrote: "I have come to the conclusion that if there is indeed a life after death, it exists only in the sense that matter does not die and also in the pantheistic conception of the eternity of nature in which I constitute a microscopic phenomenon.

"In a word, I cannot understand individual immortality. Indeed, how can we conceive of an eternal future life of eternal pleasure? In order that there should be pleasure and bliss there must be its opposite—eternal suffering. The latter I repudiate altogether. Finally, I do not even know whether one should wish for a life after death, for the only charm that life has is the alternating joys and sorrows, the struggle between good and evil, light and darkness, in a word, the unity of opposites. How can eternity be conceived as endless bliss? According to our earthly understanding we would tire eventually of bliss too, if we were altogether unrelieved. As a result of this reasoning, I have come to the conclusion that there is no eternity.

"Whilst I deny an eternal afterlife, it is with indignation that I reject at the same time the monstrous thought that I shall never see again some loved ones who are now dead. In spite of the triumphant force of my convictions, I shall never reconcile myself to the thought that my mother, whom I so loved and who was such a wonderful person, has disappeared forever and that I will never be able to tell her that even after twenty-three years of separation I still love her the same."[197]

What a profound change in our thought processes has occurred since Tchaikovsky's death in 1893! His thoughts demonstrate how, in the past, some brilliant and gifted minds have struggled with the mysteries surrounding death, dying, eternal life, and NDEs. I couldn't help but wonder what this great composer encountered when he entered the next life!

Is Jesus the Light that NDEers see when their souls, their spirits, leave their bodies? According to Scriptures, Jesus tells us He is the Light. There is no darkness at the end of the Tunnel, only peace and heavenly brilliance that defies earthly descriptions. Account after account of those who have experienced NDEs say so. Some NDEers, such as Dr. Gary Wood, were completely overwhelmed by the sight of Jesus Himself. Wood described the Light in this way: "When He looks at you, His eyes pierce you; they go all the way through you. Just love! I melted in His presence."[198]

As a matter of fact, Long found that over 40 percent of NDEers were aware of the existence of God or a supreme being, and he emphatically wrote: "The evidence from near-death experiences is that *God loves us all.* When near-death experiencers encounter God, it seems that the most common word used to describe God's appearance is 'light.'[199]

"In our earthly lives we may fear what is powerful out of concern that it could harm us. NDEers consistently describe God as powerful but often as powerfully loving. In fact, NDEers descriptions of God consistently point to the vital understanding that God is *not* to be feared but rather *embraced*."[200]

Long noted an "incredible consistency among NDErs who experience God, heavenly realms, spiritual beings, and other mystical encounters. There is an oft-quoted basic scientific principle that what is real is *consistently observed*...the consistency far outweighs any inconsistency."[201]

What else did Long discover? He found an 86 percent increase in those who believe that God exists after their NDEs, as opposed to previously. These experiences were shared with Long an average of 22 years after the NDEers had nearly died, testifying to the veracity and permanence of their memories of the experiences that they had had. "In other words, they felt confident that they were experiencing something real," Long added.[202]

In addition, Long discovered that nearly 34 percent of NDEers reported that they had entered a tunnel during their experience. Those descriptions were of a "transition place." Lin et.al. write that "tunnels and transitions seem to go hand in hand.[203] This group watched over 100 videos in which NDEers shared their experiences. As soon as the NDEers started speaking of the tunnel, their reminiscences were very brief, as they almost immediately went to talking about their attraction to the Light. This Light was at the end of the tunnel, and It defied being accurately described in our Earthly words.

"This welcoming Light ...seemed to heal their fear of death as they transitioned from this world to the next."[204] NDEers reported in great numbers that they had lost their fear of death; Linn et al. also state that "in a near-death experience, we get a glimpse of what it is like to make the greatest and most universal human transition after birth, which is death."[205]

He concludes his book *God and the Afterlife* by writing: "Here, in the investigation of the largest collection of near-death experiences to date, we see overwhelming evidence of God. This opens a door for science, for humanity, and for religion. Near-death experiences reveal that death is not an end, but an opening to a wonderful afterlife."[206]

Linn et al. note that "phrases like 'going to the Light,' 'returning to the Light,' 'healed by the Light,' and so forth have become nearly synonymous with near-death experiences and with dying. The Light seems to be a universal symbol of the realm beyond our earthly life."[207] They add that the Light, or beings of light, are central to all major religious; thus, this symbolism may color how they interpret their NDEs. Sheila Linn openly admits to never having an NDE herself. So, the Linn's' comments are based on many of those who have had NDEs.

They view birth as the first time that we pass through a tunnel, and this might serve as a "metaphor...for healing transitions, not only in that it parallels the experience of passing through a tunnel from the familiar to the unknown, but also in that it normally is preceded by the experience of being held in all-embracing love in the womb."[208] They found that a NDEer rests in a "womb-like place before he is ready to move through the tunnel and into the Light."[209]

The remarkable similarity in describing the Light is the NDEer's perception of "infinite, unconditional love, which manifests itself as light, (which) is the essence of all things, including ourselves."[210] Scientists have demonstrated that all matter consists of light, even down to the cells of our own bodies. According to one scientist, physicist David Bohm, all matter is frozen light; the basic building block of nature is light, as Bohm and other quantum physicists have discovered.[211]

Mellen-Thomas Benedict, an artist, experienced a NDE in 1982, in which he was dead for over an hour and a half, dying from incurable cancer. The reason I write about him here is simply because he came back a changed man. Ever since his adventure into the Light, he has become very involved in Quantum Biology, offering new dramatic insights about how biological systems work. Where did he attain that knowledge? From his NDE!

Since his NDE, Mellen-Thomas has obtained six patents and has added to the science of Quantum Biology by sharing his new-found knowledge about high speed healing, akin to med beds that operate at different frequencies. Consciousness groups in the world today are promoting the use of such beds to cleanse the body of disease and ailments. Mr. Benedict utilized his journey into the Light by discovering that living cells respond quickly to being stimulated by light.

---

Both Dr. Ring and P.M.H. Atwater have studied Benedict's NDE and attest to its veracity after meeting with him personally. In his initial description of the NDE, Benedict warned that his perceptions of human nature and world conditions followed him into the next life. "I perceived all humans as cancer, and that is what I got. That is what killed me. Be careful what your world view is. It can feed back on you, especially if it is a negative world view. I had a seriously negative one. That is what led me into my death. I tried all sorts of alternative healing methods, but nothing helped.

"I did not want to be surprised on the other side,"[212] Benedict had read and read about others who had experienced death, as well as about other religions and philosophies. I will let his words speak for themselves as he writes about his NDE:

"There was the light shining. I turned toward the light. The light was very similar to what many other people have described in their near-death experiences. It was so magnificent. It is tangible; you can feel it. It is alluring; you want to go to it like you would want to go to your ideal mother's or father's arms. As I began to move toward the light, I knew intuitively that if I went to the light, I would be dead.

"So as I was moving toward the light I said, "please wait a minute, just hold on a second here. I want to think about this; I would like to talk to you before I go.'

"To my surprise, the entire experience halted at that point. You are indeed in control of your near-death experience. You are not on a roller coaster ride. So my request was honored and I had some conversations with the light."[213]

---

The conversation took place via mental telepathy, and Benedict learned countless things of which he had no prior knowledge, only unanswered questions he had wondered about before his death. The light "was the most beautiful thing I had ever seen. I just went into it, and it was overwhelming. It was like all the love you've ever wanted, and it was the kind of love that cures, heals, regenerates.

"The light seemed to breathe in me…it was as if the light was completely absorbing me. The love light is, to this day, indescribable. I entered into another realm…and became aware of something more, much more. It was an enormous stream of light, vast and full, deep in the heart of life. I asked what this was.

"The light responded, 'This is the RIVER OF LIFE. Drink of this manna water to your heart's content. So I did. I took one big drink and then another. To drink of life itself! I was in ecstasy. Then the light said, 'You have a desire.' The light knew all about me, everything past, present and future.

"Yes!" I whispered. I asked to see the rest of the universe; beyond our solar system, beyond all human illusion. The light then told me that I could go with the Stream. I did, and was carried through the light at the end of the tunnel."[214]

What he then experienced was a whirlwind tour of all the creations in the universe, too detailed to explain here. But suffice it to say that he learned, in that tour, that "Every sub-atom, atom, star, planet, even consciousness itself is made of light and had a frequency and/or particle. Light is living stuff. Everything is made of light, even stones. So everything is alive. Everything is made from the light of God; everything is very intelligent.

---

"The light explained to me that there is no death; we are immortal beings. We have already been alive forever! I realized that we are part of a natural living system that recycles itself endlessly. I was never told that I had to come back. I just knew that I would. It was only natural, from what I had seen.

"I don't know how long I was with the light, in human time. But there came a moment when I realized that all my questions had been answered and my return was near. When I say that all of my questions were answered on the other side, I mean to say just that. All my questions have been answered. Every human has a different life and set of questions to explore. Some of our questions are universal, but each of us is exploring this thing we call life in our own unique way."[215]

However, not all NDEs are positive experiences. Even Benedict's contained an element of darkness. He explained: "I had a descent into what you might call hell, and it was very surprising. I did not see Satan or evil. My descent into hell was a descent into each person's customized human misery, ignorance, and darkness of not-knowing. It seemed like a miserable eternity. But each of the millions of souls around me had a little star of light always available. But no one seemed to pay attention to it. They were so consumed with their grief, trauma and misery. But, after what seemed an eternity, I started calling out to the light, like a child calling to a parent for help. Then the light opened up and formed a tunnel that came right to me and insulated me from all that fear and pain. That is what hell is."[216]

Most NDEers state that pain "abruptly returns" after their NDE ends. Some researchers have injected endorphins to see if drugs could induce visions similar to NDEs. Their attempts have

---

not been successful. [217]You may wish to return in your reading to the end of Chapter III where I discussed new studies on the use of psychoactive drugs to better understand NDEs.

Researcher Nancy Evans Bush explains that one out of every five NDEs involves "terrifying traumatic experiences such as black, cold voids, total sensory deprivation, yawning chasms of loneliness, prowling monsters, or indeed visions of an actual Hell, the description of which can vary wildly from person to person."[218] Those terrifying NDEs are too gruesome to discuss here. But if you are so inclined, look for Matthew Botsford's book titled *A Day in Hell; Death to Life to Hope*, Bill Wiese's *23 Minutes in Hell*, or (atheist) Howard Storm's *My Descent into Death*.

Storm was definitely very shaken by the experience; he wrote that some dark "figures" led him down a dark tunnel where they slowly and "with much relish…were biting and tearing at me. This went on for a long time. They did other things to humiliate and violate me which I don't talk about."

Storm collapsed under their relentless attacks, and he surprised himself by praying desperately. The hideous figures became angrier with him, and they shouted, "There is no God!" As he shrunk into a fetal position on the ground, he felt himself being pulled away from the attackers and placed back into his earthly body.[219]

The documentary *The Lazarus Phenomenon: A Glimpse of Eternity* features, in detail, two people who saw hell in their NDEs before being relieved of the visions and having the NDE

---

turn into heavenly views. The first is that of Daniel Ekechukwu, a pastor in Nigeria. In 2001, he died in a horrific accident.

Harboring ill feelings toward his wife following a nasty argument which had preceded the car crash, Daniel left his body and saw earthly humans trapped in agony, not being able to communicate with others. The fleshy bodies were not bloody in this hellish vision, with no flames or fire. However, they were eating themselves in perpetual, painful cries. His Guardian Angel was guiding him, advising him that "You reap what you sow," and that he should find forgiveness in his heart for his wife.

Then, on the other extreme, Daniel was ushered to the Gates of Heaven, where he saw structures made of no earthly substances; they seemed to vibrate and move in a flowing-type motion. Flowers within the Gates were "singing." He knew the NDE lasted for quite a long time, because the very next time he saw his physical body was over three days after his death, which was verified with a signed death certificate displayed in the video.

How did his NDE come to an end? Since the death of Daniel, his wife had spent her time reading Scriptures, and her eyes became fixed upon the story of Lazarus being raised from the dead. She convinced many from the church congregation to pray over her husband's body before he was buried in his casket. Indeed, at the funeral, or memorial service, as some call it, they removed the body from the casket, and laid hands upon Daniel's death-ridden body. Several minutes passed before breath returned to the body, and Daniel became totally aware of those around him. His first thoughts were that he must forgive his wife or God would not forgive him. And that he did!

The second true story narrated in *The Lazarus Phenomenon: A Glimpse of Eternity* takes place in New Zealand, where a heathen named Ian McCormick describes his NDE after being stung repeatedly, and fatally, by several jellyfish. During a night time diving incident, he experienced an "electrical feeling" that shook him in the water. He realized he had become entangled with a poisonous jellyfish.

His friend was able to help Ian return to the inside of the boat, and he returned Ian's dying body to the shore, hoping to get help. Rather than wait, Ian garnered some strength, probably through an adrenalin rush, and stumbled into the nearby town. There he was judged as just another drunken sailor, and refused help by a taxi driver and a Chinese man near his hotel. Both men refused to call for an ambulance, as Ian's condition worsened with the poison paralyzing him.

Finally, a friend recognized Ian, and an ambulance rushed him to the hospital. He heard a voice tell him, "If you close your eyes, you shall never awake again." Then he saw an image of himself as a young boy, followed by an image of his mother. She told him to pray, but the self-proclaimed heather had forgotten the words to any prayer whatsoever. He asked for forgiveness for the sinful life he had led, and immediately the words to the Lord's Prayer appeared in front of his eyes.

The words were personalized for him specifically, as they froze on the words, "…and forgive us our trespasses, as we forgive those who trespass against us." An inner voice urged him to forgive both the taxi driver and the Chinese man, who both had laughed at him and refused to help him.

He died upon arrival in the hospital, and entered a dark place where an evil presence told him to "Shut up! You deserve to be here." Ian was able to place his hand through his body, so he realized that he was no longer alive in physical form. Looking for an escape from the darkness surrounding him, as well as the approaching evil presence, as he described it, Ian eyed a brilliant hole just above his head.

He felt himself being lifted toward the radiant light, "like a speck of dust being drawn into a circular opening." Thereafter, he saw a tunnel drawing near him, as he cast his eyes downward at the darkness below. His form experienced "warmth, with a living light going through me." The "pure white radiance" moved through him, and all he felt was love and acceptance, regardless of all the sins he had committed. He admitted them all to the Light, which looked like the "face of God."

The Face moved aside so Ian could view heavenly, sparkling, wonderfully illuminated pastoral scenes, which he termed "Paradise." Why wasn't I allowed to be here all the time instead of going to earth?" he asked God nonverbally.

"I have no reason to be on earth," he said. "No one is there to love, and no one loves me either."

The Voice responded, "If you wish to return, God is Light, and in Him is no darkness at all." Thereupon, he envisioned his mother, still alive on earth. He realized that he could not put her through burying him, and he also recognized that the Voice was the very same Voice that had spoken to him on his way to the hospital. He decided to return.

The doctors in the room were amazed at the return of life to his body. His first "thought" was to ask the Voice, "What have I become?"

The Voice replied," You are a reborn Christian and the blood of Jesus washed away all your sins." Needless to say, Ian has led quite a different life since his NDE. Dr. Kent Richards is quoted as verifying these two NDEs in *The Lazarus Phenomenon: A Glimpse of Eternity,* in conjunction with his study of over 300 other NDEs. Richards himself had an NDE 26 years before this documentary was filmed! He quipped: "These NDEs are not even close to hallucinations, and not close at all to a dream. They are much too highly structured and ordered."

Other negative NDEs are even more horrific. They feature the darkest darkness, continuous, tortuous anguish, and the deepest desolation, with no regard to faith, religion, or culture. I will keep the faith, since I would MUCH rather dwell on the Positive, and on the Light! Or, as Isaiah 5:20 warns: "Woe to those who call evil good, and good evil; who put darkness for light, and light for darkness."

Marisa St. Clair writes: "…many people fail to report negative NDEs because they see them as punishment, or a comment on their moral status, and are often simply ashamed to tell anyone about them, let alone a researcher intent on publishing the details…being too frightened to remember the unpleasant or horrific NDE."[220]

In her initial research into NDEs and soul mates in 2001, Jody Long found a huge number of NDErs using the words "love" and "spiritual" interchangeably. "The more love they felt, the more spiritual the experience. Religion was considered the routine, social structure and practices of a group. However, spirituality lacked the dogma associated with religion. Instead of words and habits, it is the actual feeling of love and the conscious exercise of free will to bring one closer to God." You can read the entire text by Jody on the NDERF website. The document is titled "Near-Death Experience, Religion, and Spirituality." Those observant readers who know something about the "Oxford comma" will raise their eyebrows because by separating "Religion, and Spirituality" by commas, Jody indeed it telling us that NDErs consider the two terms separate entities altogether.

Another researcher into NDEs, psychologist Tony Lawrence, describes these experiences in this way: "There seems to be a general lack of cultural factors determining the content of these experiences. People from many different cultures will describe meeting a figure of light. They do not meet Jesus or Vishnu or Buddha—although afterwards they may sometimes describe what they saw in that way. The cultural influences only seem to emerge in the interpretation of what was seen, not in the basic experience itself."[221]

Actress Sharon Stone "saw the light" in 2001 when an artery near the base of her brain ruptured. She shared her NDE on several TV shows, detailing how she traveled toward a bright light and met some of her dead relatives and friends.[222]

At a meeting of the International Society of Near Death Studies (ISNDS) in San Diego in 2015, reporter Amy Wallen had the opportunity to interview two attendees. One had seen the Light and one had not, a mere indication that not everyone who has a NDE sees the Light. Beverly Brodsky described it as "a light switch goes on and you understand what it's all about. Your understanding of darkness is diminished, and you no longer fear death."[223]

The other person whom Wallen interviewed was Dave Thomas, who had a different kind of "light" vision. Dave had seriously contemplated suicide, the result of deep depression. In the process, as he pondered jumping off a bridge, he saw "angels, spirits and guardians on the Other Side," which he called His "energy." These angels, his "spiritual bros," were full of unconditional love. He labeled his main angel "his goddess," and described her as the "Starbucks Goddess."

Wallen, of course, later Googled "Starbuck goddess," and found that she is a mermaid, a siren. The website used the following description: "She stands unbound, sharing our stories, inviting all of us to explore, to find something new and to connect with each other. And as always, she is urging all of us forward to the next thing. After all, who can resist her?"

It surely seemed that Thomas reflected this Google description as he was told by the "Starbucks Goddess" and the others in the Spiritual realm that "we called you over (to go to the Other Side) because a big Spiritual Shift is about to happen, but come to think of it, you could really do some good work on earth for us." So, he experienced what Wallen called "NDE Lite."[224]

Perhaps this experience, besides showing us that no two NDEs are completely alike, suggests that "a big Spiritual Shift" is about to happen. Others at this ISNDS asked, "What is about to happen?" The answer: "A shift from the head to the heart: We will all learn to be more loving, accepting and giving." Let us hope those words ring true for all of us!

A unique quotation discovered in my research includes the words of Marisa St. Clair: No matter Who is the Light, "what really matters is the light itself, which is 'full of good things' and bestows unconditional love and healing for body and spirit," the dominant force on the Other Side.

Kimberly Sharp, founder of the Seattle International Association of Near-Death Studies (IANDS), the largest and oldest group of its kind, experienced the Light in 1970. She collapsed on a sidewalk outside an office in Shawnee Mission, Kansas, with no pulse and no breathing, despite efforts at reviving her, as CPR was performed by an EMT passer-by. "But I wasn't there. I was on a journey, the most fantastic of my life.

"The Light was brighter than hundreds of suns, but it did not hurt my eyes. I had never seen anything as luminous or as golden as this Light, and I immediately understood it was entirely composed of love, all directed at me. The Light was directed at me and therefore through me; it surrounded me and pierced me. It existed for me." She communicated with the Light telepathically, nonverbally, "learning the answers to the eternal questions of life"[225]

Sharp hesitated to share her testimony until 1985, fearing that its content would hurt her professional career as a social worker. The mission imparted to her from her NDE kept resonating in her mind: death holds nothing to fear. In her own words: "I had an increased sense of invulnerability and the absolute belief in the special importance of my life. I was braver, boldly seeking out adventures that in the past would have intimidated me. I was more willing to 'go with the flow' and accept people - even people very different from myself - as they were. Material possessions became far less important; instead, I craved new knowledge, new experience."[226]

Like others who have experienced NDEs. Sharp saw herself as transformed, looking at everything "with new eyes, strange coincidences wove themselves into the fabric" of her everyday life, and her sense of mission was reinforced. "The damnable thing about a near-death experience is that most, if not all of it, is ultimately ineffable. There are simply no words in any language to adequately express what happens to our consciousness when we die, or almost die."[227]

In an article on the NDERF website, written by Daniel Nieman, several descriptions from NDErs describing the Light were detailed. "Mary's" account is strikingly similar to that of Kimberly Sharp. Nieman comments on it: "It's interesting how she describes this Light as a "giant field or energy." She describes this field of energy as radiating and embodying unconditional love. She seems to intuitively know that this is God, the source of all existence. For a time she becomes a part of the Light, as if absorbed by it. Then she becomes a distinct consciousness again, but feels that the Light is part of her. The Light is in us and we are in the Light. She realizes how everything is interconnected because everything is a part of this one Great Light!" (!!!)

Another NDEer told Nieman there was "all the time in the world." Thus the Light existed in timelessness, eternity, in which past, present, and future existed simultaneously! Someone named "Phillippe R" described "the Light...as infinite, timeless, and unchanging. Creation is just a play, given power by the Light, the ground of all existence. Once the play is finished, we go back to this Light, which is our true Home. There we know all things and exist in a state of perfection. This life is but a play that we have created in order to experience part of our infinite possibility. It won't last forever, but the Light, with infinite wisdom, love, and compassion, is always there and waiting for us to return, as we are pieces of this great Light."

Nieman summarizes another account of "Daniel A" in this way: "What knowledge is revealed in the Light? Quite simply, All Knowledge. The light holds all knowledge; everything that ever was, is, or will be is known by the Light. The Light is the source of all possibilities and is ultimately in control of all that happens...in all the chaos of the world, there is an underlying order to it and that from this higher perspective, everything is perfect. It is only because of our limited perspectives and knowledge that we see imperfections in the world."

For quite some time, I have wondered if a fourth dimension does, in fact, exist. So many NDE accounts, as well as case studies by leading mediums and psychics, many of them Christians, I might add, seem to indicate that a fourth dimension is only a breath and a heartbeat away. Could that explain why so many people can sense the near presence of their loved departed ones? Are NDEs solid evidence of a fourth dimension?

Well, I turned once again to the website that contains more NDE information than any other: NDERF. And sure enough, Jody Long researched this very topic in an article titled "The Fourth Dimension and NDEs." She states that 774 NDEs occur in the United States on a daily basis, and they are "typically described as profoundly spiritual experiences...glimpses of the fourth dimension and perhaps not so far removed from science as we normally think."

Long revisits a book by Dr. A.T. Schofield, published in 1888, in which he uses analogies of one, two and three-dimensional worlds to theorize about a fourth dimension. Let me merely summarize it here by writing that Schofield said we can communicate telepathically in the fourth dimension, a dimension where we cannot use our physical ears.

Perhaps the Light exists in a fourth dimension in which God communicates with us telepathically, nonverbally? Many NDE accounts support such a viewpoint. One example is the account of Crystal McVea.

Hospitalized with pancreatitis, McVea "died" for approximately nine minutes on December 10, 2009. Medical personnel worked on her body tirelessly, trying to restore her breathing and heartbeat. During that time, she entered Heaven, feeling "completely infused by God's brightness and His love." She was actually in the presence of God. He answered any and all questions she had for Him. The single most compelling question she had was "Why didn't I do more for You?"

Thoughts and answers seem to flow effortlessly between McVea and God. In her own words, "I realized He IS love." Along with two angels and God, she moved down a tunnel, "a magnificent passageway of blinding, swirling, shimmering brightness. At the end of the tunnel there was a burst of an even brighter light—more intense and more vivid and more golden and more beautiful than all the other brightness…a trillion times whiter than the whitest white you've ever seen or could imagine."

Instantly, she knew it was the gates of heaven. He communicated to her that once she passed through those gates "you cannot come back." Although she wanted to stay with Him, He showed her an image of a girl three years old frolicking with a golden basket filled with a magical brightness. Unbelievably, God allowed her to see herself through His eyes, when she herself had been that little girl!

As she heard her name being called around the perimeter of her earthly body, she realized that she was about to return from her NDE. Much to the relief of her mother, whose voice

McVea had heard, the people in the room saw her eyelids fluttering.

"All of a sudden I knew I had to let her know where I was. 'I need to tell my mother I'm okay,' she told God.

"And God responded, 'The choice is up to you. Tell them what you can remember.'"

She did, and recorded her memories and how they changed her life in her book, *Waking Up in Heaven: A True Story of Brokenness, Heaven, and Life Again.*[228]

# Chapter V

## Lessons to be Learned

Of all the author's works I have studied in writing this book, Erica Brown's is the only one that somewhat disagrees with Elizabeth Kübler-Ross's "stages of grief." Brown claims that inspiration, not acceptance, is the final and most powerful "stage." Brown adds that once we realize that we need to be prepared for death, we will experience "a flood of change…that enables us to face death without fear."[229]

In her work, *On Death and Dying*, Ross listed the five stages we endure as we deal with death. They are denial and isolation; anger; bargaining: depression; and acceptance. She termed them "defense mechanisms," coping mechanisms that help people cope with very difficult situations as they face terrible news, such as the death of a loved one. Ross noted that patients who accepted their state of dying passed on within 24 hours. These patients had conversed with their doctors with words such as "I guess this is it," or "Doctor, I think I have had it," or "I think this is the miracle—I am ready now and not even afraid anymore."

However, the work of Kübler-Ross and her vast contributions to the study of thanatophobia are beyond comparison to anyone else's. She asserted that science (particularly science AND technology) has contributed to our fear of destruction and therefore our fear of death. When she witnessed her patients describing what awaits us in the next life, she, as a scientist, was stunned. How could patients who were blind describe such a beautiful, colorful, and magnificent spiritual world they have "seen" in exquisite terms when they had never had vision of any kind in the physical world? How could patients who were missing limbs report that they had regained all their limbs in their near-death experiences?

In trying to get some answers, Kübler-Ross wrote: "If [the NDE] was just fulfillment, those blind people would not be able to share with us the colour of a sweater, the design of a tie, or many details of shape, colours and designs of people's clothing. We have questioned several totally blind people and they were not only able to tell us who came into the room first and who worked on the resuscitation, but they were able to give minute details of the attire and the clothing of all the people present, something a totally blind person would never be able to do."[230]

In addition, Kenneth Ring and Sharon Cooper in *Mindsight* wrote about more than 20 patients who were blind, yet they could detail NDEs "indistinguishable from those of sighted persons.[231]

As so many other scientists and doctors that I have researched in this book, Ross was driven to read and research all that had already been written about the subject. As a matter of fact, in writing her book *On Life after Death*, she consulted 197 references, which she listed fully in her bibliography! She concluded that death does not really exist! Her text is so fascinating that I am including some of it here:

"Death is simply a shedding of the physical body like the butterfly shedding its cocoon. It is a transition to a higher state of consciousness where you continue to perceive, to understand, to laugh, and to be able to grow. Not one of the patients who had had an out-of-body experience was ever afraid to die. At the moment of this transition, you are never, ever alone. You are never alone now, but you don't know it. But at the time of transition, your guides, your guardian angels, people whom you have loved and who have passed on before you, will be there to help you. We have verified this beyond a shadow of a doubt, and I say this as a scientist.[232]

Ross affirmed that our "tunnel" is culturally determined. For her, who had an NDE, it was a "mountain pass with wild flowers simply because my concept of heaven includes mountains and wild flowers, the source of much happiness in my childhood in Switzerland."[233] Noting that none of us should fear death, she said that "...dying is feared because of the accompanying sense of hopelessness, helplessness, and isolation."[234]

Her patients were quoted many times as saying after the tunnel they had approached a source of light. Ross herself had this similar experience: "I myself experienced...an incredibly beautiful and unforgettable life changing experiences. This is called cosmic consciousness. In the presence of this light, which most people in our western hemisphere called Christ or God, or love, or light, we are surrounded by total and absolute unconditional love, understanding and compassion...we are unable to experience any negative emotions."[235] Just as no two snowflakes are alike, the energy pattern or soul of everyone is unique, said Ross.

"Watching a peaceful death of a human being reminds us of a falling star; one of a million lights in a vast sky that flares up for a brief moment only to disappear into the endless night forever. To be a therapist to a dying patient makes us aware of the uniqueness of each individual in this vast sea of humanity. It makes us aware of our finiteness, our limited lifespan."[236]

Ross studied more than 20,000 people who had NDEs. She explained that "the dying experience is almost identical to the experience at birth. It is a birth into a different existence.

"It might be helpful if more people would talk about death and dying as an intrinsic part of life. Just as they do not hesitate to mention when someone is expecting a new baby."[237]

Mediums, who have spent a great portion of their lives communicating with spirits, also firmly believe in providing a pathway for people to heal from the pains of losing a loved one. Hollister Rand affirms that mediumship presents evidence (names, cause of death, relationship, career, personality, favorite hobbies, and other information) from spirits to the aggrieved so that the aggrieved can feel confident that the departed soul is at peace. "Saying what needs to be said and hearing what needs to be heard—these are two gifts mediumship offers to the bereaved on Earth."[238]

Looking once again at the work of cardiologist Pim Van Lommel, we see that his patients expressed life changes following their NDEs. He interviewed the patients five days after cardiac arrest, two years later, and then eight years later. What were their long-term changes, if any, and what lessons had they learned?

Here's how Van Lommel summarized their changes: "…after eight years , people with an NDE scored significantly higher in the following areas: showing emotions; less interest in the opinion of others; accepting others; compassion for others; involvement in family; less appreciation of money and possessions; increase in the importance of nature and the environment; less interest in a higher standard of living; appreciation of ordinary things; sense of social justice; inner meaning of life; decline in church attendance; increased interest in spirituality; less fear of death; and increase in belief in life after death. These different levels of change are a consequence of the NDE and not of surviving a cardiac arrest."[239]

What did Greyson learn from all his studies on NDEs? He lists seven items:

1. NDEs are common experiences that can happen to anyone.
2. NDEs are normal experiences that happen to people in exceptional circumstances.
3. NDEs usually lead to several profound and long-lasting aftereffects.
4. NDEs reduce fear of death.
5. NDEs lead experiencers to live more fully in the present moment.
6. NDEs raise questions about the relationships between minds and brains.
7. NDEs raise questions about the continuation of consciousness after death.[240]

He concludes the final lines of his book by writing: "NDEs can also transform those who read about them and can ultimately, I believe, even help us change the way we see and treat one another."[241]

———————————————

Researcher Kenneth Ring agrees with Greyson's perspective. He sees NDEs as having lasting and profound effects on those who have experienced them."You never recover your original self. That is lost to you. It's not your physical body that has died, but something in you. You won't be the same again."[242] Ring views NDEs as "teachings." Furthermore, he writes: "These experiences clearly imply that there is something more, something beyond the physical world of the senses, which, in light of these experiences, now appears to be only the mundane segment of a greater segment of reality (1980)."[243] I concur!

Sabom's studies led him to believe that NDEers ended up in a "separated self" wherein communication (with others around them as they entered the Other Side) was impossible. He wrote: "During the out-of-body episode, people would experience an amazing clarity of thought, as if they were alert and fully awake, not in their physical body...as if he was questioning or evaluating his own perception of the reality of the situation."[244]

As noted earlier, NDEs happen to people from all races, creeds, and walks of life, but the core experiences is always remarkably similar. Some details may vary, based on various cultural expectations of the dying individual. Yet the effect of all NDEs can be summed up in one word: *love*.[245] Jeffrey Long reviewed over 500 NDEs from dozens of cultures and countries around the world and he too discovered "impressive similarities in the content of these NDEs."[246]

What are some of the lessons we should learn from all this NDE information?

Jonathan Cahn would perhaps answer: "Your days on earth come around only once in an eternity...only once. Every moment you have, comes around only once in an eternity...and never again. Every moment is a once-in-eternity moment, a one-eternieth moment. Therefore, every moment is of infinite value...infinitely priceless. Then how must you live? Appreciating every moment.

"Therefore make the most of every moment. For it will never come again. Whatever good you would do, do it now. Treat every moment as if it was infinitely rare and of infinite value...because it is. For every moment, and your life itself, comes around only once in an eternity.

"You have to die to go to heaven. So the key is to die. But the secret is, don't wait until you die in order to die. If you do, you'll never know the heavenly life until this life is over. But there's a way to die now even while you live. Die to your old life, and you will enter the new. Die to the flesh, and you'll live in the Spirit. Die to the earthly, and you'll enter the heavenly. Learn the secret of living in your afterlife now. It's as simple as dying and going to heaven....when the old life is finished, a new life begins.

"And so when all has passed away, the old world and everything in it...He who led you through this life will lead you in...into the Promised Land. He who held you, who kept you and who never left you...in every moment of your earthly journey...and who loved you before you were...will be with you every moment...to the end...and beyond the end...forever."[247]

# Chapter VI

## "I" Witnesses

How does science, or medicine for that matter, explain the blind being able to see after a NDE? Or how about an Oneonta, NY, surgeon, who had survived a lightning strike, suddenly acquiring an overwhelming drive to become a pianist? Yes, in 1994, Dr. Anthony Cicoria, age 55, had a NDE when lightning came out of a nearby phone booth and knocked him to the ground. When asked about this unexpected career change, Cicoria remarked, "As Mozart said, it comes from heaven." He realized that there IS life after death: "Whatever we are, our consciousness goes with the spirit."[248]

Others, who are "I" Witnesses to life after death, defy any efforts to be singled out and counted one-by-one; many of them have written books about their journeys and made music with their words. Some of their books are referenced at the end of this book for your consideration. Out of the hundreds of "I" Witness books that have been written about NDEs, those that I have read and personally recommend for your reading, are indicated by a checkmark in the list of References.

National Geographic dedicated nearly an entire issue in 2016 to the topic: "The Science of Death—Coming Back From the Beyond." It includes stories such as that of a toddler named Gardell Martin, who fell into an icy stream and was certified as dead for more than 90 minutes. Another portion of the feature article shows Linda Chamberlain, founder of the Arizona-based cryonics firm named Alcor, hugging the container that holds her husband's body, supposedly in suspended animation. Of course, that presents another question: Is her husband Fred dead?

Furthermore, the article pictures orthopedic surgeon Tony Cicoria, mentioned above in this chapter. Remember that he was struck by a lightning bolt that traveled from a nearby pay phone into his head, leveling him to the ground and thereby stopping his heart.

Some of the stories included involve patients who are brain dead and, according to their doctors, would not be alive physically if it were not for life supporting machines hooked up to them.[249] Were these patients alive? Were they experiencing the same types of near-death journey similar to Dr. Eben Alexander's? Were their souls in suspended animation?

In the course of writing this compendium of information regarding NDEs, one strange feature reared its head when several of my friends volunteered to share their near-death experiences with me. As a note of caution, some of their testimonies to be included in the following pages may not meet the definition(s) (or your definition) of a near-death experience, but they insisted that they did. So, as a reminder, a near-death experience occurs during or near *clinical* death.

Clinical death takes place after an individual's heart stops beating, as well as breathing. Usually, clinical death lasts less than six minutes. The primary reason we hear so much more in today's world about NDEs is simply the fact that doctors can revive more individuals who are clinically dead through employing ever-improving technology, training, and equipment.[250] Not everyone who has been revived from clinical death has an NDE. Only about 40 percent do.[251] As stated earlier in this book several times, not everyone's NDE is completely the same, although there are many similarities, in most cases.

---

Should you wish to review some of the best definitions of a Near Death Experience that I could find in my research for this book, consult pages 25 and 26.

The following testimonies are accurately recorded below, with only minor editing corrections. More important than anything, of course, is the content.

### Testimony of Gail L. Maholick, Lehighton, PA

"In the summer of 1959, I was 8 years old when our cousins came to visit. We were excited to be allowed to go swimming in the Parryville Dam, about a mile from our house. We, my brother, Barry, sister, Chris and cousins, Gloria, Robert, Vane and Debbie walked down Fireline Road with our inner tubes in our arms. My brother was 13and was in charge of the group.

We went in the water and I decided to sit on the top of the one inner tube with my feet dangling in the center of the tube. My cousin Gloria was inside the front tube pulling me. Somehow I slid through the center and remember thinking I was drowning.

I remember the warmth of the white light surrounding me and feeling so wanted. It was a comforting experience when suddenly, I found myself on the shore with my brother yelling at me. He said that I should have stood up, that the water was shallow and not over my head.

I felt briefly disappointed because I had felt so at peace before he pulled me out and saved my life.

Sadly, I could not save his, as he committed suicide when he was 43.

## Testimony of Paul Magargal, Roseto, PA

"Back in December 2016, I had gone through my divorce and was out on my own. I met a girl through our weight loss group; she was struggling with her husband at the time and had a drinking problem. We started seeing each other. That got her mind off the abusive husband.

She moved in with her mother, along with her two girls and her son. Things were going good, and we were making plans for the future. Then, around Thanksgiving, she said she wanted to try dating because she had never dated. She had married her first husband when they had their son, but it didn't work out. She got divorced and married an alcoholic and had two girls.

The night she said she wanted to date me and date others I was watching her kids, and actually wrote a note and was going to ask her to marry me. That went up in smoke. She dated me and another guy. We had already had plans for Christmas with the kids. She said we were still keeping those plans.

So, I watched the girls Christmas Eve Day, and we put the kids to bed and did the Santa stuff. I knew that Christmas day the girls were going to their dad's, and she had to work. Then she was going to the guy's for Christmas dinner. I was going to go home and be alone and that would be the first Christmas that I wasn't seeing my two kids.

Well, we got up Christmas morning, did the presents and all. And she started a fight over, I don't know what; her mom and I both said not to fight in front of the kids. She then told me the last eight months meant nothing, and I was nothing but someone to fill a void.

I then went home, wrote a note to her and my ex-wife and my kids, telling them I'm sorry but I could no longer handle life. I was going to end my life. Being a former Emergency Medical technician, I knew how many pills to take and a few beers and I'd be gone. I then decided that I just wanted to sleep through it all. I took only half the pills intended and drank a beer and I was out.

I was supposed to go to Christmas dinner with my roommate at his ex-wife's, another friend from weight loss group. He tried to get a hold of me. But before I fell asleep, I posted on Facebook 'Merry Christmas to all, and to all a good bye,' instead of ...to all a good night.'

A few friends from my high school days were concerned, and they started calling folks to get a hold of me. They finally got in contact with Stacey, my roommate's ex, and they had her and the police come to my house. I was found unresponsive, and almost dead.

They took me to the hospital, and I stayed in ICU for two days, asleep and on a breathing machine and IV. I remember seeing the so-called white light, and saw my mom and uncle, who already were in heaven.

I finally woke up, and the doctor said, "You knew what you were doing, and if you would have taken the rest of the pills, you would not have survived."

I am embarrassed and hurt that I let life issues and my depression drive me to that point. But the only thing I think that saved me was God wasn't done with me yet.

The light was just a bright light and I felt like I was being sucked into it. I remember feeling like I was floating, if that explains it. The experience gave me a different outlook to appreciate every day and every moment and make it count for good, because it can be gone in a blink.

When I'm down and out, I realize that taking my life isn't the solution, but it's OK to seek help. I can now talk to others and help them. You can use my name because, who knows? Someone I know may read this and may reach out for help. And maybe I'll save someone who is down and out like I was."

### Testimony of Kurt "Phillip Wazowski," Lehighton, PA

"During the Presidential campaigns of 2016, I was watching television campaign news (Hillary was doing a really annoying speech), and, suddenly, I felt what could be described as a thumb pushing on the right side of my chest. Then I started feeling very light-headed, and my right arm started to hurt.

I tried to stand up, but ended up on the floor. I had just enough strength to drag myself up the stairs to the bedroom. I tried to stand up, but fell again to the floor, this time in the bedroom. I managed to smash open an aspirin bottle because the stupid ass child proof lid wouldn't come off. I ate four of five aspirins and washed them down. I seemed to remember this was a good idea, but I kept blacking out and ending up flat on the floor.

Knowing bed was good, I got into bed and laid down. Meanwhile, I was fighting for every breath, and that seemed to be worse than the pain I was having now in my chest.

I laid on the bed on my back and I started to feel very light-headed, like I was floating on a raft in a lake. The feeling Accelerated, and I realized I had to resist, so I started with the Lord's Prayer and asking not to go yet. I wasn't ready.

Then I started seeing grainy color images of my young childhood, like fishing with my father. The images were on a, believe it or not, cartoonish wooden frame, like Hanna-Barbera drew it.

I forgot to mention I threw up as soon as I got in the bathroom.

As the images faded in and out, I was feeling the light floating feeling, and if I didn't resist it, the feeling accelerated like being pulled. I remember screaming I was not ready.

But I wasn't a floating feeling in any particular direction. It was more of a loss of mass, like I was now weighing a pound floating.

I did not see a light, but there definitely seemed to be someone or something controlling the floating feeling.

When I resisted, it responded. Anyway, I woke up around 8am, which was perhaps 9 hours after the incident began.

I ended up at St. Luke's Hospital and had heart surgery four days later.

Another time I was body surfing in North Carolina with my brother and his friends in the Atlantic Ocean after a Nor'easter. (Not smart!). I got sucked out so far I could barely see people on the beach.

Everyone was standing watching, but nobody could help. I couldn't touch bottom, and I was starting to get tired.

I suddenly felt a very warm temperature change (yeah, yeah, like I was floating into whale pee!), and something pushed me. Then it pushed me again.

After the third or fourth time, it stopped, but a wave came in that shoved me clear back to the beach. My brother was stunned, but he didn't know the whole story. I was getting that light feeling, like I did with my heart attack.

I don't know what shoved me. Maybe a dolphin, maybe a guardian angel? I was more concerned about keeping my face over the waves than what was going on under water.

So, I've had that accelerating light feeling twice, once when nearly drowning, and after my heart attack."


## Testimony of Gale Sue, Lehighton, PA

"Below is a picture of the accident I died in. I'm still in the car in this picture. It had to be towed from the building before they could extract me. I died in that car. And, I asked God that I could come back. He agreed because my work wasn't done on Earth. I don't know what I'm supposed to do, but for some reason I feel compelled to share this with you.

The car accident took place in 2017. I did have a death experience, in which I was told these things that I will write about.

I can tell you what I saw now, I saw it, exactly, as it is described in the Lord's Prayer (Thy Kingdom Come, On Earth As It Is in Heaven) I did not see any tunnels or lights or, even, people. I heard a rush of voices of familiar people that told me things past and present and experienced a peace that was so peaceful there are no words to describe it on Earth. I heard a voice that said I come to you as these people, because those are the voices you will recognize, not my own.

I heard my Mom, who died in 1997, my great Aunt Ka, my grandmother, because she raised my mom and she died in 1981. I also heard other friends and relatives, that have passed, and some that didn't pass, yet (which you would think would have been confusing, but really somehow just made sense.)

What I saw was Earth without the buildings, cars, and man-made structures. It was 1:00am when I had my accident, so it was very dark out, but somehow the mountains, stream, trees were illuminated by a soft white, peaceful glow that made them all visible. It's so hard to describe because like I said it's nothing I had ever experienced on Earth. The extreme sense of peace that flooded me was the one thing that remains vividly in my thoughts.

My son thought I tried to commit suicide because I never turned the wheel. Apparently, I drove straight into the building. Just seconds before my accident, I saw deer up the road from the skating rink building that I ran into. Everything went white after that. I heard my grandmother say to me, 'You're going to be in an accident, but it's going to be okay. You will not feel any pain. You are going to be told some things and you will be born again, if, you choose.'

I felt the accident and I heard a voice say get out of the car and go to the bathroom before the ambulance comes because you won't be able to go once 'they' (what I knew meant the ambulance) arrives. I tried to open the driver's door, but I was pinned in the building.

So, I 'believed' I crawled across the passenger seat and out the passenger window. At that point, I didn't see anything but two trees behind the skating rink. I walked to those trees and there was no car, no buildings, no people, just me and (a presence of 'a boy I thought I remembered hearing died in a car accident the year I started 9th grade in real life' But, I can't remember the boy's name. He was a cousin of a friend of mine, whose home I stayed at most of that summer between 7th and 8th grade) I believe he was from Boyertown, PA.

This boy started coming up on the weekends, and he was kind of like my first boyfriend. I think he was 16, and I was 13. And, I had forgotten all about him until at that moment in my accident. I couldn't remember his name, but I recognized him by his presence.( I had heard, like a year after that summer we hung out together, that he had died in a car accident; as the years went by, I forgot all about him and until this day I still don't remember his name.)

It was at that point that I heard a rush of voices, telling me memories, past events, the way of the world, God's Words. Then, I was asked what I wanted to do. Stay or go back? I wanted to come back to take care of a child I was tending to for the last year prior to my accident. I heard a powerful voice tell me, 'They're coming; you must hurry and get back into your car. Do you hear the ambulance in the distance? That's them. They are coming for YOU! Get back in your car and wait for them, but don't say a word until I wake you!'

That was Thursday morning at 1:00 am... it seemed like forever, and I continued hearing the rush of voices until Sunday morning when I woke up in the hospital in Philadelphia. You can see the actual accident with the car. I never climbed out of the car because both doors were pinned between the cement blocks of the building until the tow truck pulled my car out of the skating rink and the jaws-of-life cut me out of the car. But, I will swear I climbed out of that car and heard, felt and saw the above.

Side note: I did not have a seatbelt on. It had been broken the year before, and I never had had it fixed. 17 days later I was released from the hospital with not a physical mark on me.

Believe me, I realize how insane this sounds and, even I cannot fully digest it. As you have probably already noticed, I have a hard time piecing everything together. About two weeks before my accident, something started happening to me.

I would start writing a post or comment or a response on Facebook and all of a sudden it was like I no longer had control of my fingers and thoughts, like it was some kind of spontaneous writing. I never had anything happen like that before or since my accident. I think I need to do a little back explaining.

I had been in a great relationship for 18 years until 2012. I was overworking myself. My son had just gotten married and moved to North Carolina. At the same time I discovered my daughter was in drug addiction for opiates. And, I had a complete mental breakdown. One thing led to another and I was put on medications, the strongest being Adderall for a diagnosis of ADHD. Through the course of the nervous breakdown I destroyed my relationship and found myself alone looking for a place to live.

I reached out to two bad characters, who I ended up living with, one in 2013, and the other I met in 2016, to get away from the first. The 2nd one's son moved back in the house with us, and his 13 month old daughter, named Ava. I would watch Ava from 4:30 am until 9:00 pm. When her dad was finished working his actual job at 4:30 pm, they'd come home, eat dinner I had made, and go out in their garage to work on their race cars until 9:00 pm, while I was watching the baby. (This is the child I asked God to come back for, because I knew she wasn't taken care of by them.)

I was on SSI because of my breakdown. They took all my money each month, used my car to travel to work and wherever else they wanted to go while I was taking care of the baby every day and night from October 2016. Three months after my accident, my son's father, Robert Barilla, helped me get away from them by finding me my own house, helping me move and get back on my feet. I hadn't dated Robert since 1986. And, I think I had only seen him a few times, the last being our son's wedding in December 2011.

My son found out I was in the accident on Sunday, 3/14/17, and he and his wife and kids drove up from North Carolina to claim me in the hospital. The guy I had been living with never reported me missing or notified my family, even after finding out on Friday, 3/12/17, that it was me in the accident.

He was the whole reason I was in my car that night. I thought he was in diabetic shock. He was sleeping next to me and moaning loudly. I couldn't wake him, which had happened about 6 times previously during the year I lived with him. I'd get up: go get his test kit. Check his blood and determine where his levels were so I knew if he needed orange juice or insulin, which I would also give him to bring him around. That night he didn't have test strips.

I had woken from a deep sleep to get the test kit for him. When I realized he didn't have test strips, almost instinctively, I got dressed, got in my car in Forest Inn, headed to Walmart to buy test strips, but hit LaRose's Skating Rink instead. I believe my accident was a Godsend to get me out of that house and away from those people. In fact, there's no doubt in my mind.

However, because I was on Adderall since 2012, I came up positive for drugs and got a DUI as a result of that accident. I was going to fight the charges, but I didn't have the money. The Defense Attorney told me I would have to pay for professional witnesses, like doctors and scientific lab technicians, to explain the breakdown of Adderall. Like, I said, the guy I had been living with used all my money, I was on SSI, and I only had liability on my car. So, it was out of the question. I took the DUI.

I swear to God, I was not on drugs besides my legally prescribed medication at the dosage I was prescribed. I do not drink, and since that accident I am no longer on any medication. I am back to work for the last 2 1/2 years and I have never been more sure about anything in my life. I was not injured in the accident, yet, it put my entire life back together better than before.

My daughter is clean 1 1/2 years. I'm engaged, working, and have the best life imaginable. I had prayed and prayed for a miracle to get out of the mess I had been in. And, then, that accident happened, which has made me a better person and given me a second chance at life. And, it was God that did this all for me. There is not one shred of doubt in my mind.

I'm sorry if this sounds so crazy. All I can give you is what I know happened to me. What I was told. How it was told to me. . and what I was told to do next for myself… and to encourage others. Free will decides others' fate, as it has mine.

On my arm, I got a tattoo 3 years before the accident, spontaneously… it states the words I have always lived by in Gaelic: God, Family, Love, Integrity, Humility, Dignity, Righteousness, Responsibility until Death. Right after that tattoo,

I had gotten the Celtic Woman Warrior Tattoo on the inside of that same arm. I chose each of those things to get tattooed on my arm out of the blue one day. In, afterthought, I often wonder what made me do that.

I started out writing this as a post for Facebook, but I decided not to post it. But, I'd like to share it with you. I'm not crazy, but this is truly what I saw and learned. I was told to follow God's Law in the 10 Commandments. And, the Bible is a history book of the accounts of the time.

I'm not an overtly, religious person. But, I am a firm 'Faithful' person. Faithful to God and the 10 Commandments. I believe the Bible, Quran and other such text, were written by men about the things they saw and predicted (from the behaviors of their societies during their time). It's not hard to believe or predict there will be wars when people value greed over integrity. Basically, the Bible, Quran and other texts are "history books" of the accounts and predicted outcomes if people don't change their behaviors! And, they outlined how behaviors are supposed to change.

God gave us two things: free will and The 10 Commandments, 10 simple rules to follow, and the choice to follow them or not. People try to bargain with God all time. Please give me this. Please give me that. I pray I hit the lottery. Please save my family member. Please let me get that job. Please don't let us go to war. But, God never promised this life would or wouldn't be pain free and would always be easy.

He gave us free will to make the correct choices, choices to follow His Commandments, even when faced with great tragedies. And, even, as we watch others receive things we, in our own understanding, perceive as great blessings.

What are the moral choices you make? Are you envious and jealous? Angry or hurtful? Or, are you humble and grateful, even, for others that seem blessed beyond you? Do you bear false witness (lying, rumors, gossip, encouraging others to hate because you do?) Or, do you covet thy neighbors' goods? (steal, cheat or lie for your own benefit because you value material things over your soul?)

OR, do you forgive, forget and keep moving forward the best you can, no matter what earthly hardships you believe you are faced with? We find it really easy to say what we would do in someone else's shoes, but what do you do in your own shoes, in your own blessings and hardships? Because, I can tell you, firsthand, mind your own business and live for your own soul because in the end, the choices you have made are the ONLY ones you will be judged on.

I can pretty much predict we will be at war. Not because I'm a prophet. But, because I happen to know, Afghanistan and Pakistan are the only places on Earth that are rich with lithium, also where it is closest to the Earth's surface, making it easiest for First World Nations to mine. Lithium is used in batteries (computers, cell phone batteries, car batteries, medicine and everything else used to run the world today.)

I know this because I know Hillary Clinton revealed that the US was in Afghanistan and Pakistan because we wanted to build roads and develop their countries so we could get the mineral rights to their lithium, while she was at a press conference in Brazil right before she stepped down as Secretary of State (which she was forced to do because she revealed that information).

Am I a prophet? No. I was paying attention. Like a detective, you have to listen to the small details to get the big picture! So, will there be wars? Absolutely. Because how do you convince a country of people who don't want their land touched or their beliefs of how to live, that you want to go strip them of their resources (be it oil, lithium, or anything else?) You make it about human basic rights, or religion, or morals and values.

So, now, Biden gave the lithium rights to China... the country that needs that lithium to produce cell phones and computers, TVs, medicine, etc... at the cost of human lives! He also just gave the miners' rights to the oil in the Middle East to Russia, who is building a pipeline through Eastern Europe while stopping our own pipelines, making us dependent on Russia and China. (Any of this sound familiar?) Because it's not rocket science!

Why you ask? Greed. Political Greed! The politicians and major corporations will profit, while they distract us with things like hating each other. They will never stop abortions! They could care less who's gay or lesbian, but they use those things to divide us on moral grounds so they can deceive us at the highest levels. That is the bottom line!

Was Trump a hero? Yeah, he kind of was. He wanted to bring industry back to America so we would be competitive against China, who now makes everything. But, that would cost a lot of money. Money to put mills back in operation. Money to make people go back to work. Money to have the electric to run those mills. Money to develop our country to make us a self-sustaining nation once again. And, all politicians would rather make money bargaining with other countries for self-serving purposes, rather than spend money rebuilding a self sufficient nation that they cannot profit from. Even, at the cost of human lives (which they can use to keep people divided on how things should have happened, instead of the way they did).

Haven't you ever wondered why India is never in a war? They have the largest population, but no real army? Because they don't have natural resources and Buddhism. Live humbly and at peace with nature! They don't mind living poorly because they know it is not materialistic things that save their souls. That frees them to become better learners in medicine, technology and life. If they become blessed in this life, it is because of that education. So be it, they are grateful, but they will never be dependent because they live this life for the next, unlike, Christians, Muslin and Jews. Or, America, China and Russia. Buddhists mind their own business!

They say things come in 3's. 3 world powers: America, Russia and China; 3 major world religions: Christians, Muslims, Jews; 3 major sources of power: electric, oil, natural resources. Will there be wars? As long as people keep deceiving and exploiting their fellow men. Will people die? Yes, until someone comes along to stop the deception. Will we see the Bible play out? Absolutely, because history repeats itself until we learn from it!

Am I a prophet? Nope! I chose criminal justice because I wanted people to stop hurting one another. But, in such, I became a trained observer. I observe what is going on and I put it together, like, I'm sure others have in the past. Religion, governments, Hollywood, and even scientists have stopped many of those people? Through movies about conspiracies, viruses, depressions, assassinations and attacks on people's character, e.g.: President Trump, for the sole purpose of greed!

Spoiler Alert: We're all being played and it's costing human lives. What do we do next? What is the right thing to do? And, how do we change it? As an individual, nothing. But, as a world full of people, maybe we can make a difference!

PS: I'm not super religious because I'm of the belief that organized religions made by man started off with the best intentions, but, like everything man has his hands in, religion gets distorted, manipulated and corrupted. But, I am faithful to God.

I don't take my every waking hour in prayer because I don't believe that's what God wanted. I believe He sends us messages from time to time and at those times we're supposed to acknowledge and thank Him for His guidance. And, then, we're to go about our day trying to live as God wants us to.

If God truly wanted us to be religious 100% of the time, He would have kept us in Heaven. But, He sent us here to experience being human, which, in itself is an amazing gift.

I don't even go to church... but, I do believe God gives his messages to regular people (all people) in ways they understand. The key is for all people to pay attention to their message and spread God's Word in ways they understand.

Sometimes, I believe that makes people sound crazy. And, sometimes, people get fanatical in their attempts to share their message, which makes them sound even crazier.

But, my message to you (Joe) is to collect each message you receive from God and people for your books, do your best to decipher them in the order you feel most important. You have the gift of writing given to you by God."

## Testimony of Theresa DaCosta Keiser, Lehighton, PA

"When I was only 6 months old, I had a terrible case of the flu. The doctor treated me with aspirin, until one day I hit my father's head, on the other side of the room, with projectile vomiting!

He said enough was enough, and I was admitted to the hospital. Tests showed that had I not gone there, I would have died within 45 minutes. A blood clot had developed in my heart, but the doctors were able to dissolve it somewhat. It moved to an area in my arm later in life, and even today I experience deterioration of my bones, due to this flu episode and how it was treated initially.

Ever since that time, I have had dreams of people who are *going* to die. Until now, I have been reluctant to share this information, since many people may think that I am simply making this up. But, that is not true!

One time I saw an image of a person whose name I couldn't recall, but shortly afterwards his name did come to me: on the exact day and time that he actually died. I was alarmed.

Then, another time, I was selling Avon products, when a customer called me to say that a Snowman and Snowwoman that she had purchased from me did not play the music it was supposed to. Unfortunately, the items could not be returned, but I asked her to 'give it to somebody,' while I placed an order for a replacement.

Several days later, this customer, who was my sister's neighbor, had a stroke. I felt so bad for her. I gave the lady a rosary, which I had from Medjugorje, and told her to pray, and that I would pray for her too.

The night before this lady died, the song, which would not play from the broken Snow items, kept playing in my dreams.

Of course, these are only two examples of when this has happened to me. There are many more.

I keep thinking that these dreams are the result of my near death experience when I was a child. Only God knows..."


### Testimony of Laurie Dunbar Nothstein, Tamaqua, PA

"When I was walking on a sidewalk July 1, 2014, I was hit by a car, out of nowhere! I was airlifted by helicopter to a hospital in Bethlehem.

They gave me 7 painkillers for the excruciating pain. As the copter arrived at the hospital, I went into cardiac arrest, plus organ failure. They kept working on me.

They were able to bring me back, but not before I saw the white light and my best friend. She had passed from cancer, and she held my hand and said, "It is not your time."

I know it was a few minutes that they had used the paddles on me to try to resuscitate me. I was bedridden for a month and a half. Twelve specialists said I would never walk again.

I had a broken tibia, fibia, soles of my feet, left ankle, as well as both feet being crumbled. I ended up with total knee replacement, but I *am* walking since the surgeries.

I am in acute pain, but I'm here! Yes, you can still have life threatening issues every day, but I cope with it each and every day."

### Testimony of Mel Sharbaugh, Lehighton, PA

"My near death experience took place 23 years ago. I died after giving birth to my son, and I will never forget what I saw.

I had lost so much blood that they took me into surgery to stop it. All of a sudden, I was out of my body, floating on the ceiling. My back was against the ceiling. I was looking down on them working on me!

I could hear everything they were saying, and I remember the time on the clock was 12:30 am. Then everything turned black. I couldn't see anything, just heard them talking.

Then I saw a small dot of light in the total blackness. I wasn't walking towards the light; it was like I was on an escalator, but not going up steps. It was going straight.

Along each side of me, I saw black and gray silhouettes of people. The black ones were taller (like an adult), and the smaller ones were gray. I could hear me flat line, and the nurses saying, "We are losing her."

As I got closer to the light, I couldn't hear anything more, and I reached out my hand to the light, and boom!!! I was awake in recovery.

It took me a long time to tell my Mom, because she was an atheist, and I thought she would think I was crazy. I couldn't believe that when I told my Mom, she *did* believe me! She said from having 2 C-sections something went wrong, because I was in surgery way too long.

When they called 'Code Blue in the OR,' she had run to the nurses' station to see what was going on, and she heard them saying that **I** was Code Blue!

I don't know what that light was at the end of that black tunnel, but it sure was beautiful! Thank you for reading my story. It's something I don't tell just anyone, until now!"

## Testimony of Brian Kromer, Bowmanstown, PA

"Thirty years ago, I woke up in the morning to go trout fishing with my wife. We got all of our stuff together and went to a creek. The day went well with no fish, but the time spent together was great!

We decided to go get a bite to eat at a restaurant. While in the restaurant, I developed a severe ringing in my ears and a very bad headache. I told her I was going outside for a smoke. I gave her money to pay the bill.

After I went outside, I hopped in my truck and started rubbing my neck and head. The ringing in my ears sounded like very loud cicadas. I felt like if I slept I would feel better?

I said out loud, "If there's a God, please let me see my wife one more time." She came out the door and I smiled. There was sharp pain and blankness…it felt like I was in a long nap.

I kept hearing a noise saying, 'Wake up.' My body was very tired, so I couldn't wake up. It came again. 'Wake up!' So I listened to it that time, and I opened my eyes.

Standing in front of me was a minister giving me my Last Rites. I learned later that my family had pulled the plug on me two hours earlier!

The following year was hectic: I had 3 strokes, woke up with a scar on my chest, and had a hole in my heart that they had to seal!

Then I found out that I was in a coma for a year! I had to learn how to walk and talk all over again, and how to move my hands, etc. I don't know what that voice was, but I would hear it again down the line...

Skip 12 years of my life and one night I was watching football. It felt like I was having a heart attack. I lost my wife from before, but had a new fiancé.

I was throwing up, couldn't talk, etc. They rushed me to the hospital, but I was in too much pain that I passed out. Same blackness and that voice, 'Get up!'

It happened twice in my life, so this time I opened my eyes and there was a nun speaking over me. This time I was in a coma for two weeks. I found out who the voice was... it was my deceased grandfather.

There was a feeding tube in me because of pancreatitis. Like 5 minutes later my body kicked. I felt something shock me.

I heard, 'Get up!' and found out later that they had declared me dead. I am a survivor, and I am here to tell you that after blacking out, you should 'GET UP!'

King of weird that each time I was 'dead' I opened my eyes to see religious people by my side! Really weird!!!"

## Testimony of Carol Fleshman, Edmond, OK

"I had a near death experience on April 29, 1989. Although it was a long time ago, it is in my mind like it happened yesterday.

I had an ectopic pregnancy that was missed by several doctors and I nearly died. The pain was intense for five days. On the fifth day, I went to Deaconess Hospital in Oklahoma City, where they confirmed that my tube had burst. Besides, I was bleeding internally.

Sometime during or after emergency surgery, I left my body. I saw my body there in the bed and a bright light near the door. It was like a hole in the ceiling.

When I opened my eyes, the nurse was screaming for help with a code of some nature. The following morning, when my mother arrived at the hospital from Illinois, she said I was as white as a ghost.

What I do remember is that it happened so fast! I was not afraid. No words were spoken, only the very bright light that was waiting for my next move.

Then, On July 2, 2000, I was in the very same hospital. I had had an open Nissen fundoplication surgery on July 3. I had complications. I had tubes everywhere.

I kept hearing this pecking noise on my window in the room. I was in a bad way. I called for the chaplain. I knew the devil was near, and I refused to allow him in with all the fear I had going on, as I was alone during that time.

The chaplain came, but not before a still small voice spoke to me and said it is done. I'll never forget that!

From that moment on, I knew that God was indeed real, and with the experience I had in 1989 He has sealed my faith. God is so good. He has never failed me!"


## Testimony of Ron, Las Vegas, NV

One account related to me is that of a Las Vegas resident named Ron. His experience took place at the age of 19, while he was serving in the US Army in 1972.

While lying on his bunk in the Army barracks, Ron prayed deeply, asking to be in God's presence. He then entered an area of "green fog," as his brain collaborated with God, and everything around him "slowed down."

Ron described his experience as "God's computer was plugged into my brain." Since that time, he has discovered that others have had similar experiences, including pastors and other Christian friends.

Who am I to judge? As I have seen throughout my research into this topic, despite all the "I-Witness" accounts, some who have explored this topic still dispute the authenticity of NDErs. Their accusations include that some people may have simply experienced a "high" similar to that induced by drugs or deep religious fervor. I will not join ranks with the doubting Thomases.

In conclusion, Ron agreed in his talk with me that not all NDEs are the same. He humbly asked that I include an applicable Biblical passage here. It is as follows: "It is doubtless not profitable for me to boast. I will come to visions and revelations of the Lord. I know a man in Christ who fourteen years ago—whether in body I do not know, or whether out of the body I do not know, God knows—such a one was caught up to the third heaven. And I know such a man—whether in the body or out of the body I do not know—God knows—how he was caught up into Paradise and heard inexpressible words, which it is not lawful for a man to utter. Of such a one I will boast; yet of myself I will not boast, except my infirmities. For though I might desire to boast, I will not be a fool: for I will speak the truth. But I refrain, lest anyone should think of me above what he sees me to be or hears from me." 2 Corinthians 12: 1-6, under a heading "The Vision of Paradise"

Since I have had an NDE myself, I can relate to others who have shared their testimonies with me. I can also relate to the thousands and thousands of others worldwide who have reported their very own NDEs to others. As the Biblical verse above reminds us, we are not fools.

### Testimony of Sam Flores, Poway, CA

"My first near death experience was when I was around five years old. One day my youngest sister was sick with a fever, and my mother had given her some St. Joseph orange-flavored aspirin. I'm sure you remember those!

Anyway, I saw where my mother had put the aspirin away in the cupboard in the kitchen, and when no one was around, I climbed up the countertop and found them, and decided to eat the entire bottle. I also ate a half a bottle of Bayer aspirin. I didn't care for the taste, which is why I only ate half the bottle.

When I had finished and started to place the empty and half-consumed bottles back, I noticed that my second oldest sister was watching me; she threatened to tell my mother, but I begged her not to, not knowing that the outcome of my situation would be much worse than any punishment from my mother.

Needless to say, my sister told my mother, and she became hysterical! I was rushed to the hospital just in the nick of time. The doctors stuck hoses down my nostrils and throat, and they pumped my stomach, along with charcoal that they had administered. It was a horrible experience that I vividly remember and will never forget.

As I've gotten much older and have become a Born Again Christian, just about nine years ago, I think back about that day and know that Our Father God was looking over me and decided that He had a plan for me here on this earth. I'm still waiting for the sign as to what His Will shall be. Since then, I have been serving Him.

I had another such experience when I was around eleven years old. I didn't actually see anything, but I absolutely felt His Presence. He allowed me to have the physical strength to save myself. This indeed is my second near death experience, but this one contains what I have come to recognize as Divine Intervention.

Yes, I was much older than my first experience, so I remember it as if it happened yesterday! I was walking home from Little League Baseball practice around dusk. I had to cross a double set of railroad tracks in order to get to my neighborhood.

As I got closer to the railroad tracks, the warning lights started to flash and the bells started to sound, indicating that a train was near. At that moment I tucked my glove into my rib cage and made a beeline towards the tracks to try and beat the train so that I wouldn't have to wait for it to pass, or possibly wait longer if it stopped for any reason.

I glanced to my right and noticed the headlight of the train, and it was a lot closer and traveling a lot faster than I had anticipated. So, I increased my speed! As I approached the first set of tracks, I leapt over the first rail, and as I was leaping over the second, my foot hit it and I stumbled forward, blearing the track.

However, I fell onto the next set of tracks, where both my thighs happened to land with blunt force, impacting me right on the first rail, instantly causing extreme pain.

As I laid there in excruciating pain traveling through my legs, I turned my head towards the direction of the train and noticed that it wasn't on the set of tracks that I has just crossed and tripped over, but instead, on the tracks that I had just fallen on!

Immediately, I went into panic mode, and then shock. I tried to move my body, but I couldn't; my legs were rendered useless. I was incoherent with fear. At that moment, I uttered the words: 'Dear God, Please Help Me."

In an instant, I felt a divine presence fill my entire body, and suddenly I was rolling over the tracks and cleared them just feet away, right before the train passed. I laid on the ground for what seemed like an eternity, and then attempted to get up. But the pain in my thighs had not yet subsided.

I slowly started to raise myself from the ground still in pain from the fall. At that moment, I heard a loud voice in the distance asking, 'Hey, kid, are you OK?'

A concerned gentleman had witnessed what had happened, and got out if his car to come to my aid. I told him that I was OK and thanked him for his concern. He then told me to be more careful and left.

When I finally arrived home with sore legs and walking gingerly about the house trying not to call attention to myself, I went straight to the bathroom and took a shower, and started to cry as I stood in the stream of water. I thanked God for saving me.

For decades thereafter, I had never shared my experience with anyone, not even my mother. I truly believe that the Good Lord is definitely watching over me."

### Testimony of Joseph Cortese, Henderson, NV

"Now for my own testimony…it may pale in comparison to other NDEs; it is true. It simply takes some of us longer to digest and understand the NDE, and then open up with others about the experience. Many others may feel that their NDEs will not be taken seriously, or that they may be subject to ridicule or negative criticism by the doubtful, if they should detail their personal experience.

Mine took place in the late 1990s. To save money, and also to learn how it is done, I, along with a friend of mine who was an experienced roofer, replaced the asphalt shingles on my ranch room during the hottest part of Pennsylvania's summer, July. It was quite an undertaking, but it taught me a lot.

We had cast the old shingles onto tarps on the front lawn. In order to keep the grass alive, my next order of business was to get the old materials off the lawn. Luckily, through the kindness of a neighbor who had a trucking delivery service, I was loaned a 10 ton dump truck overnight. He was to pick it up the next morning, and dispose of the shingles.

I arose very early the next morning, at dawn's early light, to discover that the task I was to perform would be nearly impossible if I could not lower the tailgate of the truck. The truck was parked with its rear to the front of my two-car attached garage, with no keys to automatically raise the bed, or open the gate. Thus, I struggled to throw the heavy shingles over my head and into the truck bed a few at a time. I had only a few hours before the truck would no longer be available for my use.

My watch and the quickly rising sun told me that I was taking much too long. I would have to find another way. What about jumping inside the truck and trying to open the tailgate with a sledge hammer, without raising the body of the truck? After all, it seemed that after I would loosen the two chains that were holding the top ends of the tail gate, I would be able to move past any rust or metal that might remain, and thereby lower the gate.

However, the tailgate did not respond to the hammering I was giving it from inside the bed, and I worried that I would wake up the neighbors if I continued. I resigned myself to the situation and resumed my work on the ground, tossing a few shingles into the truck at a time. I had no sooner thrown a few more into the truck and turned around to pick up some more, than the tailgate decided to leave the upright position and slam down on my head and back; I had pivoted, and managed to turn slightly away, as I saw what was coming and could in no way stop it.

I was down for the count. I realized that I was unconscious, and not in my body. I felt no pain. Later, I discovered that the eyeglasses I had worn at that time were shattered, but I do remember trying to rub my eyes, as if what I was seeing was a mirage of some type.

There it was: the tunnel, brightly illuminated and lined with relatives who I knew were deceased, particularly some of my aunts and uncles. Their flowing, white garments covered all of their bodies, except for their recognizable faces. I could not believe my eyes. As I floated into the tunnel a bit more, I saw an intensely bright, pulsating Light at the tunnel's end.

Before I could float any farther, I felt like I was being stopped, like someone had jammed on the brakes in a car to avoid an accident, and I could hear the lined relatives repeating, 'You are not finished, Joe. You have to go back.' It was then that the vision ended, and I realized I was back inside my body, enduring intense pain.

Blood was streaming down my face and over my eyes from a cut on my head, but I couldn't see anything because my glasses were uselessly broken. I knew that my wife and daughters were still inside the house sleeping, and the chance that they could hear me or had any clue as to what had happened was zero. Besides, window air conditioners and fans were running inside their bedrooms.

I used all the energy I could muster to shove the 300 pound tailgate off my back and crawl slowly toward the open garage. Yes, I had been pinned to the ground. The entire neighborhood was still asleep. Thank God I could get free from the crushing weight on top of my neck and upper back.

Once inside the garage, I had to ravel up several steps to get inside the kitchen. It was a laborious process. Attached to the kitchen was the living room, which was separated from the bedrooms by shuttered doors. I could see that the doors were still closed, and by that time I was running out of energy.

In shock, I could barely mumble, much less shout for help. I collapsed on the rug just inside the room, when I heard one of the doors open. My wife noticed that I was hurt, and she expressed dismay on how she would get the blood stained carpet cleaned. In total frustration, I managed to utter one word, 'Ambulance,' before I blanked out into unconsciousness.

She must have called 911. When I was awakened by two EMTs, who shook me and knew me by name (One was a former student of mine, Donna, by the way.), the next thing I felt was being moved onto a stretcher and juggled into the ambulance. On the way to the hospital, I faded in and out of consciousness, hearing Donna encouraging me to hang on, that everything would be OK.

In the ER, my father appeared, and held my hand as they checked the extent of the injuries. After a few hours, I awoke inside a hospital room with IVs and monitors all over the place it seemed. I asked for my chiropractor, a close friend who had worked on my neck and spine many times following a previous accident. (On my way to work years earlier, my car had slid on black ice, right through a stop sign and into a tree.)

It wasn't long before the Doctor arrived and told me that he had read the x-rays. I felt paralyzed; he said that the shock to my body had caused that reaction. His diagnosis: despite the trauma to my head, neck, and upper spine, I had missed death by 1/8 of an inch. Any farther and my neck and spine would have been separated!

After a few stitches on the head and several days of physical therapy to relearn how to walk, I was discharged. With the assistance of pain killers, my family and I were able to keep our vacation plans that we had made before the accident. I was happy about that because I did not wish to cancel those plans and deny the family a getaway.

Never did I tell them, or anyone else for that matter, about my NDE. My curiosity told me to begin reading and researching the Near Death Experiences of others, which I have done for many years. It has helped me cope with the thoughts and feelings I have kept inside for so long.

With the COVID outbreak, the Spirit (a still, quiet voice inside my head) kept telling me to write this book and share its information with others. So many people have faced death since the outbreak began."

++++++++++++++++++++++++++++++++++++++++++++++++++++

The word "heaven" so far has appeared at least 26 times in the content of this compendium. Have you ever wondered: Is Heaven a place, a location, or a state of mind and being? Perhaps it is all of these! Before I end my testimony, I am determined to mention Heaven a few times more. Why?

Answer: my father, who, died one day shy of his 93$^{rd}$ birthday. In his closing days, he thought a lot about his next residence. He vowed: "You will never take me out of this house until I am dead." But God had other plans.

I spent several months being his care-giver before his final stroke would hospitalize him, and eventually incapacitate him so that he would need to be placed in hospice. However, even before that time, he had asked questions about Heaven. He wondered: "What do we do all day up there?" and "How do we all fit up there?"

During one of the last times he would attend the Roman Catholic Church in our hometown, he exclaimed, "There is no hell!" Hearing this remark nearby was the pastor, who quipped, "Oh, yes, there is. No way of denying that, Joseph!"

Of course, there is no day or time in the next life! It is Charles Swindoll who explained the concept of eternity in the most understandable terms: "If you have a steel ball, the size of this earth, 25,000 miles in circumference, and every one million years a little sparrow would be released to land on that ball to sharpen its beak and fly away only to come back another million years and begin again, by the time he would have worn that ball down to the size of a BB, eternity would have just begun."

May my Dad rest in peace, along with my many relatives and friends, who now have all the answers to these, and any other questions that they may have had, before their final breaths were taken on this earth.

# Chapter VII

## Conclusions

So, what should *WE* learn from all this? One answer is offered by hospice doctor Christopher Kerr and his co-author Corine Mardorossian, after speaking with over 1,400 patients: "Dying is an experience that pulls us together by binding us to those who loved us from the start, those we lost along the way, and those who are returned to us in the end. The dying most often embark on a hopeful journey in which they are embraced one more time by those who once gave their lives meaning, while those who hurt them drift away. Death is also a form of final justice, one in which the scales are balanced by love and forgiveness.

"As sickness begins to overtake the drive to live, there is a shift. The dying continue to cherish life, but not for themselves—for others. They express concern for loved ones, in gestures of kindness and hope, even as they say good-bye. Buried within their stories is the same awe-inspiring message, repeated again and again."[252]

Erica Brown's answer can be summarized best by quoting her: "When the end is near for us or someone we love, and the bloated carcass of our egos has collapsed, it is time to put the hurt aside and to love. Saying 'sorry' is an act of love. Forgiveness without a living path to redemption is hard to achieve, but sometimes it's all we have to offer. With our strength diminished at the end of life, love may be the only gift we have left to give. And 'sorry' may be the only word we can say. And it may be enough.[253]

---

"Happy endings must be both about the dying managing death better and the living managing the death of those we love better."[254] Brown also quotes Sherwin Nuland in describing our fascination with death: "To most people, death remains a hidden secret, as eroticized as it is feared. We are irresistibly attracted by the very anxieties we find most terrifying; we are drawn to them by a primitive excitement that arises from flirtation with danger. Moths and flames, mankind and death—there is little difference."[255]

To alleviate any pain or suffering caused by death, C.S. Lewis seemingly advises: "If we will not learn to eat the only food that the universe grows—the only food that any possible universe ever can grow—then we must starve eternally."[256] Perhaps he is referring to Love, the only permanent "food" in this life or the next!

"We brought nothing into this world, and it is certain we carry nothing out." 1 Timothy 6:7. Except love.

On the cover of Long and Perry's book, *God and the Afterlife*, authors Dannion and Kathryn Brinkley, who themselves authored a book entitled *Secrets of the Light*, conclude: "If someone asked for proof that life after death exists, refer them to this book. Dr. Long and Paul Perry have gone way beyond faith and into science, providing us with well-documented proof of what we have known absolutely for thirty-five years—there is life after death!"

Pearson concluded that "the content of an NDE cannot be attributed to expectation," what the dying person expected to see

_____

after life.[257] Add that to Nelson's conclusions: (...believing in experiences outside the brain is faith. Sensing that something is 'more than coincidence' is also an expression of faith. It's folly to expect that science can prove or disprove the truthfulness of these experiences. But spiritual hope based on *false* science is cruel. The nature of faith makes it immune to science's demands for consensus, verification, and prediction."[258]

Therefore, Nelson is telling us that we need to understand that the brain is a spiritual organ, not that the mind exists separate from the physical brain. His final words on this subject are "Such understanding will firm up our search for meaning and result in a new 'birth of freedom.'"[259]

His earlier argument declared that "the brain is nowhere near physically dead during near-death experiences. It is *alive* and *conscious*. Brain death happens by the death of cells. When lack of blood kills a brain cell, calcium rushes in, causing the cell to rupture like a water balloon being burst by a pin. Once the cell is ruptured, there is no putting it back together.

"New brain cells do not grow to make up for those that have died. The brain, as a whole organ, dies cell by cell, and when a critical number of the 100 billion brain cells reach a point where they have ruptured, and the few that might remain can't sustain life, the brain is dead. Van Lommel's near-death experience patients were not 'clinically dead'...their state resembled that of someone who had fainted."[260]

Nelson believes that the brain is the spiritual doorway to the next life. Those who experience NDEs are not dreaming;

they are not delusional, and they are not brain dead or brain damaged. They "return" very much a changed individual, as we have read about earlier.

One of the main issues that a skeptical Nelson has with Parnia's findings is his belief that NDEs and OBEs are the result of "hypoxia," more than anything else. Hypoxia is a loss of consciousness, not of life itself. Nelson parallels hypoxia with a phenomenon called REM intrusion. This intrusion possesses brain traits similar to deep sleep, "when the same brain activity that characterizes dreaming somehow gets turned on during other, nonsleep events, such as sudden loss of oxygen."[261]

Parnia, on the other hand, views NDEs as "actual death experiences," death as a "process, not a moment. 'It's a whole body stroke, in which the heart stops beating but the organs don't die immediately. In fact, he writes, they might hang on intact for quite a while, which means that "for a significant period of time after death, death is in fact reversible.'"[262]

Cardiologist Michael Sabom is also referenced in Pearson's conclusions, when she writes that he found in his research that patients who had NDEs reported details surrounding their resuscitation 80 percent better than those who had suffered a cardiac arrest without experiencing a NDE. Sabom found that NDEers "related accurate details of idiosyncratic or unexpected events during resuscitation" that they should not have been able to describe at all.[263] As we have seen in other research noted in this book, scientists and medical personnel have found remarkably similar results.

_____

Another I might add is that of Holden (2009). In an analysis of 107 NDEs, Holden found that in only eight percent of the cases did inaccuracies of the physical surroundings exist. In other words, 92 percent of the time, experiencers were able to accurately describe what was going on around them, in detail, as they were going through the NDE.[264]

Van Lommel found that those who had the deepest NDEs were more likely to die within 30 days of their cardiac arrest, in expectation of returning to the fruition of their previous journey into the next life. Pearson quotes Van Lommel, who told her that "medically, they were no different from the other patients. I cannot offer an adequate explanation for this."[265]

Similarly, Jeffrey Long concluded, from nine major lines of evidence, that NDEs are real, and that they are medically inexplicable. In his more than 35 years of studying cardiac patients and their NDEs, Long explained how electroencephalogram measurements definitively flat-lined 10-20 seconds after cardiac arrest. Since there is no significant or measureable brain activity, no "brain cortical electrical activity," a "prolonged, detailed, lucid experience following cardiac arrest should not be possible, yet this is reported in many NDEs."[266]

Of all the financially successful people that I have met and/or read about, one stands apart from all the others. He delivered a great speech, which included his observations about his impending death. I would do my readers a terrible "mis-service" if I did not include his exact words in this book. I can only urge you to watch him deliver this speech via YouTube, or any of the other social media sites.

His name: Steve Jobs, former CEO of Apple Computer and of Pixar Animation Studios. The occasion: delivering the Commencement Address for the graduating class at Stanford University. The date: June 12, 2005.

Why am I including Steve's entire speech? Simply because this speech contains such a powerful message about life and death, and not fearing either one, that its words will forever remain in my memory. As a matter of fact, had the COVID 19 pandemic *not* cancelled the 50th Class of 1970 Reunion at my high school alma mater, Lehighton Area High School in Lehighton, Pennsylvania, I would have reformulated Steve's Commencement Address for the students of the Class of 2020, of course, in the hope that I would have been invited to deliver such a speech! But that did not occur.

Biographer Walter Isaacson described the speech, which Jobs wrote on his own, in this way: "The artful minimalism of the speech gave it simplicity, purity, and charm. Search where you will, from anthologies to YouTube, and you won't find a better commencement speech. Others may have been more important, such as George Marshall's at Harvard in 1947 announcing a plan to rebuild Europe, but none has had more grace."[267] May it have a similar effect on you, my readers!

++++++++++++++++++++++++++++++++++++++++++++++++++++++++

"I am honored to be with you at your commencement from one of the finest universities in the world. I never graduated from college. Truth be told, this is the closest I've ever gotten to a college graduation. Today I want to tell you three stories from my life. That's it. No big deal. Just three stories. The first story is about connecting the dots.

"I dropped out of Reed College after the first 6 months, but then stayed around for a drop-in for another 18 months or so before I really quit. So why did I drop out?

"It started before I was born. My biological mother was a young, unwed college graduate, and she decided to put me up for adoption. She felt very strongly that I should be adopted by college graduates, so everything was all set for me to be adopted at birth by a lawyer and his wife. Except that when I popped out they decided at the last minute that they really wanted a girl. So, my parents, who were on a waiting list, got a call in the middle of the night asking: 'We have an unexpected baby boy; do you want him?' They said: "Of course." My biological mother later found out that my mother had never graduated from college and that my father had never graduated from high school. She refused to sign the final adoption papers. She only relented a few months later when my parents promised that I would someday go to college.

"And 17 years later I did go to college. But I naively chose a college that was almost as expensive as Stanford, and all my working-class parents' savings were being spent on my college tuition. After six months, I couldn't see the value in it. I had no idea what I wanted to do with my life and no idea how college was going to help me figure it out. And here I was spending all the money my parents had saved their entire life. So I decided to drop out and trust that it would all work out OK. It was scary at the time but looking back it was one of the best decisions I ever made. The minute I dropped out I could stop taking the required classes that didn't interest me and begin dropping in on the ones that looked interesting.

"It wasn't all romantic. I didn't have a dorm room, so I slept on the floor in friends' rooms, I returned Coke bottles for the 5 cent deposits to buy food with, and I would walk the 7 miles across town every Sunday night to get one good meal a week at the Hare Krishna temple. I loved it. And much of what I stumbled into by following my curiosity and intuition turned out to be priceless later on. Let me give you one example:

"Reed College at that time offered perhaps the best calligraphy instruction in the country. Throughout the campus every poster, every label on every drawer, was beautifully hand calligraphed. Because I had dropped out and didn't have to take the normal classes, I decided to take a calligraphy class to learn how to do this. I learned about serif and sans serif typefaces, about varying the amount of space between different letter combinations, about what makes great typography great. It was beautiful, historical, artistically subtle in a way that science can't capture, and I found it fascinating.

"None of this has even a hope of any practical application in my life. But 10 years later, when we were designing the first Macintosh computer, it all came back to me. And we designed it all into the Mac. It was the first computer with beautiful typography. If I had never dropped in on that single course in college, the Mac would have never had multiple typefaces or proportionally spaced fonts. And since Windows just copied the Mac, it's likely that no personal computer would have them. If I had never dropped out, I would have never dropped in on this calligraphy class, and personal computers might not have the wonderful typography that they do. Of course, it was impossible to connect the dots looking forward when I was in college. But it was very, very clear looking backward 10 years later.

"Again, you can't connect the dots looking forward; you can only connect them looking backward. So, you have to trust that the dots will somehow connect in your future. You have to trust in something—your gut, destiny, life, karma, whatever.

184

This approach has never let me down, and it has made all the difference in my life. My second story is about love and loss.

"I was lucky—I found what I loved to do early in life. Woz and I started Apple in my parents' garage when I was 20. We worked hard, and in 10 years Apple had grown from just the two of us in a garage into a $2 billion company with over 4,000 employees. We had just released our finest creation—the Macintosh—a year earlier, and I had just turned 30. And then I got fired. How can you get fired from a company you started? Well, as Apple grew, we hired someone who I thought was very talented to run the company with me, and for the first year or so things went well. But then our visions of the future began to diverge and eventually we had a falling out. When we did, our Board of Directors sided with him. So, at 30 I was out. And very publicly out. What had been the focus of my entire adult life was gone, and it was devastating.

"I really didn't know what to do for a few months. I felt that I had let the previous generation of entrepreneurs down— that I had dropped the baton as it was being passed to me. I met with David Packard and Bob Noyce and tried to apologize for screwing up so badly. I was a very public failure, and I even thought about running away from the valley. But something slowly began to dawn on me—I still loved what I did. The turn of events at Apple had not changed that one bit. I had been rejected, but I was still in love. And so, I decided to start over.

"I didn't see it then, but it turned out that getting fired from Apple was the best thing that could have ever happened to me. The heaviness of being successful was replaced by the lightness of being a beginner again, less sure about everything. It freed me to enter one of the most creative periods of my life.

"During the next five years, I started a company named NeXT, another company named Pixar, and fell in love with an amazing woman who would become my wife. Pixar went on to create the world's first computer animated feature film, Toy Story, and is now the most successful animation studio in the world. In a remarkable turn of events, Apple bought NeXT, I returned to Apple, and the technology we developed at NeXT is at the heart of Apple's current renaissance. And Laurene and I have a wonderful family together.

"I'm pretty sure none of this would have happened if I hadn't been fired from Apple. It was awful tasting medicine, but I guess the patient needed it. Sometimes life hits you in the head with a brick. Don't lose faith. I'm convinced that the only thing that kept me going was that I loved what I did. You've got to find what you love. And that is as true for your work as it is for your lovers. Your work is going to fill a large part of your life, and the only way to be truly satisfied is to do what you believe is great work. And the only way to do great work is to love what you do. If you haven't found it yet, keep looking. Don't settle. As with all matters of the heart, you'll know when you find it. And, like any great relationship, it just gets better and better as the years roll on. So, keep looking until you find it. Don't settle. My third story is about death.

"When I was 17, I read a quote that went something like: 'If you live each day as if it was your last, someday you'll most certainly be right.' It made an impression on me, and since then, for the past 33 years, I have looked in the mirror every morning and asked myself: 'If today were the last day of my life, would I want to do what I am about to do today?' And whenever the answer has been 'No' for too many days in a row, I know I need to change something.

"Remembering that I'll be dead soon is the most important tool I've ever encountered to help me make the big choices in life. Because almost everything—all external expectations, all pride, all fear of embarrassment or failure—these things just fall away in the face of death, leaving only what is truly important. Remembering that you are going to die is the best way to know the trap of thinking you have something to lose. You are already naked. There is no reason not to follow your heart.

"About a year ago, I was diagnosed with cancer. I had a scan at 7:30 in the morning, and it clearly showed a tumor on my pancreas. I didn't even know what a pancreas was. The doctors told me this was almost certainly a type of cancer that is incurable, and that I should expect to live no longer than three to six months. My doctor advised me to go home and get my affairs in order, which is doctor's code for prepare to die. It means to try to tell your kids everything you thought you'd have the next 10 years to tell them in just a few months. It means to make sure everything is buttoned up so that it will be as easy as possible for your family. It means to say your goodbyes.

"I lived with that diagnosis all day. Later that evening I had a biopsy, where they stuck an endoscope down my throat, through my stomach and into my intestines, put a needle into my pancreas and got a few cells from the tumor. I was sedated, but my wife, who was there, told me that when they viewed the cells under a microscope the doctors started crying because it turned out to be a very rare form of pancreatic cancer that is curable with surgery. I had surgery and I am fine now.

"This was the closest I've been to facing death, and I hope it's the closest I get for a few more decades. Having lived through it, I can now say this to you with a bit more certainty than when death was a useful but purely intellectual concept:

"No one wants to die. Even people who want to go to heaven don't want to die to get there. And yet death is the destination we all share. No one has ever escaped it. And that is as it should be, because Death is very likely the single best invention of Life. It is Life's agent. It clears out the old to make way for the new. Right now, the new is you, but someday not too long from now, you will gradually become the old and be cleared away. Sorry to be so dramatic, but it is quite true.

"Your time is limited, so don't waste it living someone else's life. Don't be trapped by dogma—which is living with the results of other people's thinking. Don't let the noise of others' opinions drown out your own inner voice. And most importantly, have the courage to follow your heart and intuition. They somehow already know what you truly want to become. Everything else is secondary.

"When I was young, there was an amazing publication called The Whole Earth Catalog, which was one of the bibles of my generation. It was created by a fellow named Stewart Brand not far from here in Menlo Park, and he brought it to life with his poetic touch. This was in the late 1960s, before personal computers and desktop publishing, so it was all made with typewriters, scissors and Polaroid cameras. It was sort of like Google in paperback form, 35 years before Google came along; It was idealistic and overflowing with neat tools and great notions.

"Stewart and his team put out several issues of the Whole Earth Catalog, and then when it had run its course, they put out a final issue. It was the mid-1970s, and I was your age. On the back cover of their final issue was a photograph of an early morning country road, the kind you might find yourself hitchhiking on, if you were so adventurous. Beneath it were the words: 'Stay hungry. Stay foolish.' It was their farewell message as they signed off. Stay hungry. Stay foolish. And I have always wished that for myself. And now, as you graduate to begin anew, I wish that for you. Stay hungry. Stay foolish. Thank you all very much."[268]

+++++++++++++++++++++++++++++++++++++++++++++++++++++++++++++++++++++++++++

Jobs delivered this speech about two years after his initial cancer diagnosis in 2003. He procrastinated on getting surgery for nearly nine months as he tried alternative approaches to treatment. Then in 2004 he underwent a major reconstructive surgery called a Whipple Operation.

That procedure entails removal of a part of the pancreas, along with part of the bile duct, the duodenum, and the gallbladder. The intestines are reconnected to get the gastrointestinal fluids entered into the stomach.

After a short recovery period, Steve returned to his job at Apple. Publicly, he refused to release any details about his health matters, deeming them a private issue. However, it seems that the media has a way of obtaining information that it wants to, when it wants to, so in June of 2009 the *Wall Street Journal* told the world that Jobs had received a liver transplant in April.

Again, Jobs returned to Apple, this time on June 29, 2009. As his health still declined, he took a leave of absence in January of 2011. In August of that year he resigned but became chairman of Apple. He died two months afterward.

Shortly before his death, Jobs shared these reflections with Isaacson: "I'm about fifty-fifty on believing in God. For most of my life, I've felt that there must be more to our existence than meets the eye.

---

"I like to think that something survives after you die. It's strange to think that you accumulate all this experience, and maybe a little wisdom, and it just goes away. So I really want to believe that something survives, that maybe your consciousness endures.

"But on the other hand, perhaps it's like an on-off switch. *Click!* And you're gone.

"Maybe that's why I never liked to put on-off switches on Apple devices."[269]

The media buzzed about his beliefs, religious and otherwise, as they always do when someone famous dies. Most media outlets have already prepared press releases and obituaries, as such, so journalists do not need to do their writing and research immediately upon the death of the individual.

CNN led the media coverage by commenting: "Traversing India sparked Jobs' conversion to Buddhism. Kobun Chino, a monk, presided over his wedding to Laurene Powell, a Stanford University MBA..." *Forbes* described Jobs as a "Buddhist and a vegetarian," as did Wikipedia.

But in looking at Jobs' comments about his religious beliefs, he told *Time* in 1997 that "I believe life is an intelligent thing, that things aren't random." Indeed, as Ed Stetzer wrote on his blog called "The Exchange" for *Christianity Today*, Steve's comments above indicate the complex belief system that Jobs held, a "system that extends well beyond the Buddhist teachings."[270]

---

Just a few hours after Steve Jobs died, Stetzer tweeted and blogged how Jobs "literally changed the world. Watching his health over the last few years reminds us of our own mortality—and Steve thought that death was a good thing for all of us to consider." Hence, my inclusion of this moving Commencement Speech in its entirety, not only the part about death. The speech gives us a clear picture of what Jobs truly held as his own personal belief system.

Stetzer continued: "It is a biblical thing to see life a fleeting (Psalm 89:47).

"I do not know Steve's spiritual condition, but I know that each of us must live in the light of eternity. Steve died today. I could be tomorrow. May I live my life considering that reality—that life is fleeting AND that eternal life is a gift to all that have been made new in Christ.

"You don't even know what tomorrow will bring—what your life will be! For you are a bit of smoke that appears for a little while, then vanishes" (James 4:14 HCSB).[271]

Seemingly in response to the way in which various media outlets responded to Steve's death, on the very next day after Steve's death, Stetzer added the following remarks to his blog. They are critical to answering the questions posed in this book, and I respect the eloquence with which Stetzer chose these words:

"As a believer, I appreciate the words of Paul McCain, a helpful and charitable thinker in confessional Lutheranism. His blog, Cyberbrethren, is in my Google Reader, and he is a LCMS Lutheran (a group that would be friendly with conservative evangelicalism). Paul gave additional information and some helpful suggestions:

'Unlike some of my fellow Lutherans and other fellow Christians, who felt a need at Jobs' passing to begin making pronouncements about his eternal destiny, I am not rushing to judgment. I can't help but recall Abraham Lincoln's quip, "Better to remain silent and be thought a fool, than open your mouth and remove all doubt." Can we learn from Steve Jobs' errors and mistakes in life? Of course, and we should, every bit as much as we must learn from our own. But must we, on the news of his passing, be so quick to condemn him and focus only on his faults and failings? No.
One more thing...

'Steve Jobs was baptized and instructed in the Christian faith, so we can do a bit more than talk about "common grace"; we can also hope that God, in His own ways, at times and places of His choosing, may have worked in Steve's life, at the last, a remembrance of the gifts from Christ he had received in his life. Unless you have been with a person in their last days, you have no idea what goes on in a person's heart and mind in the closing days and moments of life. Let us pray God brought back to Steve the remembrance of what he had been taught as a young man in a Lutheran church—Missouri Synod confirmation class, taught by my friend Rev. Dr. Martin Taddey, now deceased.

'So, let's leave the judgment to God, and leave the judgmentalism to those who have no hope. We who have hope in Christ know that for all mankind the One who suffered, died, and rose again as the victor over our greatest enemies: sin, death and the devil, has called us to be His very own. We hold out hope that, in His mercy, He once more reached into Steve Jobs' heart and mind at the end. And that is the "one more thing" that would be better than anything Steve ever announced and told us about.'

"As Christians we should care about these things. It matters what a person believes. But we should care about them in deliberate and thoughtful ways. I am grateful for Steve Jobs and the contributions he made. I am praying for his family. And I appreciate Paul McCain's wisdom and clarity as we process the loss of someone who made a huge impact on our culture."[272]

In Matthew 7:1, Jesus warns us: "Judge not, that you be not judged," and he proceeds to call those hypocrites who criticize and judge others without first looking in the mirror at themselves. Perhaps we would be wise to follow Jesus' advice when we hypocritically judge the works and lives of others.

It is He, the Light, who will judge each one of us when we do not experience a NDE, but rather when we experience final death in this life, and birth into an eternal one.

Perhaps we should realize that science cannot explain everything. Only God can. Independent American artist, scholar, and therapist Iona Miller advised: "All speculation about after-death conditions remains more philosophical than scientific, even when mired in the philosophy of science and the psychology of scientists."[273] She quotes Marie-Louise von Franz (1987) who noted: "It is in fact true, as (Carl) Jung has emphasized, that the unconscious psyche pays very little attention to the abrupt end of bodily life and behaves as if the psychic life of the individual, that is, the individuation process, will simply continue...The unconscious 'believes' quite obviously in a life after death."[274]

Indeed, life is a great mystery, but death is life's greatest mystery. Death may be the secret of life. Miller concludes her essay by quoting Jung: "But when we penetrate the depths of the soul and when we try to understand its mysterious life, we shall discern that death is not a meaningless end, the mere vanishing into nothingness—it is an accomplishment, a ripe fruit on the tree of life."[275]

Sabom might comment on Jung's analysis of the self as it could be applied to NDEs in this way: "During the NDEs the separated self became the sole conscious identity of the person with the physical body remaining behind as an empty shell."[276]

Most NDEers who have a belief in a happy afterlife exhibit *LESS* fear of death following their experience, which surprises some researchers (Noyes, 1979). [277] Indeed, the experiencers generally are no longer anxious to die, nor are they ever interested in committing suicide. They extend their decreased fear of death to those they love who are dying, and they seem to find the grieving process easier to handle. Since NDEers believe that there is life after death, "that the spirit, self, or mind survives," they are consoled because their dying loved one is passing on "to a painless and peaceful existence."[278]

As author Jonathan Cahn suggests, "The most important thing, no matter when it comes, is to be ready and to be right with God."[279] While we are alive on Earth, we should realize that "all things—our lives, our beings, our breath—come as gifts from God. Of ourselves we have nothing. All our notions of ownership are an illusion; all our pride, a deception. We are not sovereign but completely dependent. Everything we have—our possessions, our money, our riches, every moment of our lives—everything has been given to us.

"Every heartbeat is borrowed. Everything in this world that draws or repels us, entangles us or compels us, everything we seek after, dwell on, or live for, is temporary, fleeting, and passing away. Therefore the meaning of this life is not found in anything of this life, but only in Him who lies behind it. And the purpose of this life is not found in seeking anything of this life, but only in seeking Him who gave it."[280]

After more than twenty years of research into NDEs, Dr. Kenneth Ring was moved by the great number of those who had experienced NDEs and then share their experience to help dying patients. They described a "peace that passeth all understanding," and they are "uniquely qualified to transmit this knowledge directly to the dying person."[281]

Such also was the case of Peter Panagore. After dying during a mountain climbing event, he spent more than 20 years of his life helping the dying prepare for the next life. During his personal NDE, Panagore experienced hell, forgiveness, and unconditional love. Unlike others, he felt God inside. He did not see God.

Seeing a gateway and a tunnel was a part of his vision. He described it as "shimmering and flowing, like a waterfall, only it was not water, and was simultaneously translucent and transparent. I reached out with my being to touch the shimmer, to feel it…and I did. I touched the shimmer with something like a hand, but I had no hand. The shimmer was Alive. The gateway was Alive. I felt the Life in it. It was Living Energy. I felt the

---

energy of Life flowing in the shimmer and I felt it flow into me." [282]

Unlike the Voice described by Ian McCormick in *The Lazarus Phenomenon: A Glimpse of Eternity,* Panagore's Voice was only heard internally: "I heard the Voice of the Almighty deep inside my soul, beneath me, around me, beyond me, and the Voice filled me with my name—and, in the filling, knew me in totality."[283]

Similarly, his hell was an internalized soul experience: "It was, it turns out, the hell I had created for myself; or, rather, my own hell entered into me, overtook me, owned me, and filled me. It was my personal hell because I saw that I had created it second by second…while I lived enfleshed. I made my own hell, and it was horrifying. The hell I suffered was to see, hear, feel, understand, and embody all of the pain I had ever caused during my earthly life to anyone I had known, from their point of view. I had carried their pain with me and brought their pain with me into the afterlife.[284]

On the other hand, God gave him the choice whether or not to return. In choosing to return from Heaven, Peter was told that he wouldn't live the same life as he had. That proved to be so true! Read his book to acquire all the details. But know that Peter's advice is that "All the bits and pieces of love you have given or collected are in your soul" and these accompany you forever. The sins you have committed, or the hell you have caused on earth is forgiven. All that remains is love. "Every act of love accumulates in your soul. No one, and nothing, can take these from you or destroy them. Love is eternal, and love is inside you."[285]

In sharing my testimony and that of others in this book, I hope that you readers will understand what awaits us after we die. Each and every one of us is delegated with an important mission in this life. Whether we choose to align our minds and souls with that purpose is a choice given to us by the Light, the Source of all Love, God. We have free will, yes. Ultimate justice awaits us in the next life, and what goes around does come around. Some may call that karma, but the Biblical words warn: "Whatever a man sows, that he will also reap."--Galatians 6:7.

Death holds nothing to fear, if you have led the best life you possibly could. Perhaps Melvin Morse said it best in his book, *Closer to the Light*: "Near-death experiences appear to be a cluster of events so that one cannot understand the total by looking at its various pieces. One cannot understand music by studying the various frequencies of sound that generate each note, nor does one need to have a deep understanding of acoustical physics to enjoy Mozart. The near-death experience remains a mystery."[286]

# Afterword

## Some Famous Quotations about Death

"Fear does not stop death – it stops life." --Anonymous

"Why, do you not know, then, that the origin of all human evils, and of baseness, and cowardice, is not death, but rather the fear of death?" --Epictetus

"To die is poignantly bitter, but the idea of having to die without having lived is unbearable."
--Erich Fromm

"Death borders upon our birth, and our cradle stands in the grave." --Joseph Hall

"To die is to go into the Collective Unconscious, to lose oneself in order to be transformed, into form, pure form."
--Hermann Hesse

"As men, we are all equal in the presence of death."
--Publilius Syrus

"Man imagines that it is death he fears; but what he fears is the unforeseen, the explosion. What man fears is himself, not death."
--Saint-Exupery

"Nobody knows, in fact, what death is, nor whether to man it is not perchance the greatest of all blessings; yet people fear it as if they surely knew it to be the worst of evils." --Socrates

"Death is like a fisherman who catches fish in his net and leaves them for a while in the water; the fish is still swimming but the net is around him, and the fisherman will draw him up—when he thinks fit." --Ivan Turgenev

"God visits the soul in a way that prevents it doubting when it comes to itself that it has been in God and God in it, and so firmly is it convinced of this truth that, though years may pass before the state recurs, the soul can never forget it, never doubts its reality." --St. Teresa of Avila

"How strange this fear of death is. We are never frightened at a sunset." --George Macdonald

"Death is not the end; it is simply walking out of the physical form and into the spirit realm, which is our true home. It's going back home...We unzip the body, so to speak, let it fall to the ground and walk through the next door clothed in our spiritual form, which was always there inside the physical body."
--Stephen Christopher Dennis

"Death is the great leveler. It recognizes no rank, treating all equally." --David Jeremiah

### Some Famous Quotations about Life and Death

"We are like the phoenix. Rising again, with a new life ahead of us." --Pam Munoz Ryan

"The art of living well and the art of dying well are one."--Epicurus

"A good life fears not life nor death." --Christopher Fry

"I'm not afraid of death. It's the stake one puts up in order to play the game of life." --Jean Giraudoux

"It matters not how man dies but how he lives. The act of dying is not of importance, it takes so short a time." --Samuel Johnson

"One wants to live, of course, indeed one only stays alive by virtue of the fear of death."--George Orwell

"Oh Death where is thy sting! It has none. But life has."
--Mark Twain

"I am of the opinion that my life belongs to the whole community. As long as I live, it is my privilege to do for it whatever I can. I want to be thoroughly used up when I die, for the harder I work, the more I live. I rejoice in life for its own sake. Life is no brief candle for me. There is a soul of splendid torch which I've got hold of for the moment and I want to make it burn as brightly as possible before handing it on to future generations." --George Bernard Shaw

"This I know. All things are connected like the blood which unites one family. All things are connected. Whatever befalls the earth befalls the sons of earth. Men did not weave the web of life; merely a strand of it. Whatever he does to the web, he does to himself." --Chief Seattle

"You are loved and cherished, dearly, forever. You have nothing to fear. There is nothing you can do wrong over there."
--Dr. Eben Alexander III

"A human being is part of the whole called the universe. We experience ourselves as something separate from the rest...a kind of optical delusion of consciousness. This delusion is a kind of prison restricting us to our personal desires and affection for persons nearest to us. Our task must be to free ourselves from this prison by widening our compassion to embrace all living creatures and the whole of nature. The true value of a human being is determined by the measure in which they have obtained liberation from the self. We shall require a substantially new manner of thinking if humanity is to survive." --Albert Einstein

## Some Famous Quotations about Fear

"It is not death or pain that is to be dreaded, but the fear of pain or death." --Epictetus

"O! How vain and vile a passion is this fear! What base uncomely things it makes men do."
--Ben Johnson

"Of all the passions, fear weakens judgment."
--Cardinal De Retz

"The only thing we have to fear is fear itself."
--Franklin D. Roosevelt

"Where fear is, happiness is not." --Seneca

"Present fears are less than horrible imaginings." --Shakespeare

"F. E. A. R. has two meanings—Forget Everything and Run, OR, Face Everything and Rise. The choice is yours." --jbr0203

"Did you ever look in a mirror and not realize that the man staring back at you was your own reflection?"--Jonathan Cahn

# Appendix A*

Have you ever had a Near-Death Experience (NDE)? If so, I would like to hear from you. I would be honored if you would allow me to include your story in my third book, soon to be published. The book is titled *After We Die, Then What? A Compendium of Near-Death Experience Research & Findings.*

If you will allow me to use your material in this book, please fill out the short sentence below with your signature. If you need more space, please attach another sheet of paper to fully tell of your heavenly encounter.

**I,**

_____(printed),

allow Dr. Joseph F. Cortese to use the submitted material (story and/or photo) for use in the publication of his new book about Near-Death Experiences (NDEs). *Unless I write otherwise in the Notes section below, he may use my name in the book.*

**Signature**

_____

**Notes:**

_____

_____

**Please mail or email to:**

**Dr. Joseph F. Cortese**
**951 Las Palmas Entrada Ave Apt 1328**
**Henderson, NV 89012**
**drjoe679@hotmail.com**

**Other books by Joseph Cortese, Ed.D:**

*Phoenixivity*
*The Missing Link in American Public Education*

*This form was completed by all those whose testimonies were included in Chapter VI.

**My Story:**

_____

_____

_____

_____

_____

_____

_____

_____

_____

# Notes

## Foreword

1. Donne, J. *Death be not proud.* Retrieved from: https://www.litcharts.com
2. Thomas, D. *Do Not Go Gentle into That Good Night.* Retrieved from: https://www.litcharts.com

## Introduction

3. Alecson, D. (2021, April). This Mortal Coil: Sheldon Solomon on How Fear of Death Affects Our Lives. *The Sun, 544,* 5.
4. Ibid., 7.
5. Ibid., 10.
6. Freeman, C. (1985, July). Near-Death Experiences: Implications for Medical Personnel. *Occupational Health Nursing,* 354.
7. Op. cit.
8. Kais
er, S. (2015). *Adventures for Your Soul: 21 Ways to Transform Your Habits and Reach Your Full Potential.* New York, NY: Berkley Books, 157.
9. Ibid., 297.

## Chapter I
## Fear of Death: The Elephant in the Room

10. United States: How afraid Are You of Death? (2021, March 9). Retrieved from https://www.statista.com/statistics/959347/fear-of-death-in-the-us
11. Ibid., (2016, November).
12. Morrow, A. (2019, November 28). When Your Fears about Dying are Unhealthy. Retrieved from: https://www.verywellmind.com/scared-to-death-of-death-1132501, 1.
13. Survey Reveals Our Reluctance to Discuss Own Death. Dying Matters: Let's Talk About It. Retrieved from: https://www.dyingmatters.org/page/survey-reveals-our-reluctance-discuss-own-death
14. Ibid.
15. Holland, K. (2019, August 28). Everything You Should Know About Thanatophobia. Retrieved from: https://wwwhealthline.com/health/thanatophobia
16. Wikipedia, Death Anxiety (psychology), 7. (original source:doi: 10.2466/pms.1982.54.1.271).
17. Wikipedia, Death Anxiety (psychology), 7. (original source: doi: 10.1080/07481189608252787).

18. Wikipedia, Death Anxiety (psychology), 4. (original source: doi: 10.1080/2153599X.2016.1238844).

19. Schroeder, S. (2019, August 12). Why We Need to Talk About Our Fear of Death. Retrieved from: https://wwwhealthline.com

20. Tompkins, P. (2012). *The Modern Book of the Dead: A Revolutionary Perspective on Death, the Soul, and What Really Happens in the Life to Come.* New York, NY: Atria Books, 60.

21. Ibid.

22. John, T. (2015). *Never Argue with a Dead Person: True and Unbelievable Stories from the Other Side.* Charlottesville, VA: Hampton Roads Publishing Company, Inc., xxi, 93.

23. Mitchell, P. Retrieved from: https://www.ted.com/talks/megan_mcarthur_a_astronaut_s_lessons_on_fear _confidence

24. Morrow, A. (2019, November 28). When Your Fears about Dying are Unhealthy, 4.

25. Op. cit.

26. Open Yale courses: PHIL 176: Death/Lecture 22 – Fear of Death. Retrieved from: https://oyc.yale.edu/philosophy/phil-176/lecture-1

27. Johnston, J. Prepare for a Good End of Life. TED Talk.

28. Walker, K. What Fear Can Teach Us. TED Talk.

29. Atwater, P.M.H. (2011). *Near-Death Experiences: The Rest of the Story.* Charlottesville, VA: Hampton Roads Publishing Company, Inc., 41.

30. Kragen, P. (2014, March 19). Death Cafes Talk up Dying. *San Diego Union Tribune.*

31. Moorjani, A. (2012). *Dying to Be Me: My Journey from Cancer, to Near Death, to True Healing.* Carlsbad, CA: Hay House, Inc., 48.

32. Higgins, J. and Bergman, C. (2011). *The Everything Guide to Evidence of the Afterlife; A Scientific Approach to Proving the Existence of Life After Death.* Avon, MA: Adams Media, 94.

33. Pearson, P. (2014). *Opening Heaven's Door: Investigating Stories of Life, Death, and What Comes After.* New York, NY: Atria Books.

34. Cain, T. (2021). Are Near-Death Experiences Proof of the Afterlife? Retrieved from: https://www.beawake.com/author/tomcain, 2.

35. Tassell-N. and Lindsay, N. (2015, August 5). "I'm not afraid to die: The loss of the Fear of Death after a Near-Death Experience." *Mortality>Promoting the interdisciplinary study of death and dying, 21,* 1.

36. Timmerman, T. (2015). Why Lament a Bad Death." *The Philosophers' Magazine, 69*:44-50.
    doi: 10.540/tpm20156941, 26.

37. Van Lommel, P. (2010). *Consciousness Beyond Life: The Science of the Near-Death Experience.* New York, NY: HarperOne, 7.

38. Ibid., 8.

39. Ibid.

40. Caputo, T. (2017). *Good Grief: Heal Your Soul, Honor Your Loved Ones, and Learn to Live Again.* New York, NY: Simon & Schuster, Inc., 68.

41. Ibid., 156-157.

42. Van Praag, J. (2009). *Unfinished Business: What the Dead Can Teach Us About Life.* New York, NY: HarperOne, 45.

43. Browne, S. (2011). *Afterlives of the Rich and Famous.* New York, NY: HarperOne, 7.

44. Ibid., 8.

45. Williams, L. (2011). *The Survival of the Soul.* Carlsbad, CA: Hay House, Inc., 47.

46. Rand, H. (2020). *Everything You Wanted to Know About the Afterlife: But Were Afraid to Ask.* Hillsboro, OR: Beyond Words, 68-69.

47. Ibid., 144-146.

48. Ibid., 3.

49. Van Praag, J. (2009). *Unfinished Business: What the Dead Can Teach us About Life.* New York, NY: HarperOne, 2-3.

50. Ibid., 59.

51. Ibid., 163.

52. Ibid., 210.

53. Mann, D. and Becker, K. (2020*). Facing Your Fears: A Navy Seal's Guide to Coping with Fear and Anxiety.* New York, NY: Skyhorse Publishing, 110.

54. Ibid., 119-120.

55. Brown, E. (2013). *Happier Endings: A Meditation on Life and Death.* New York, NY: Simon & Schuster, Inc., 1.

56. Ibid., 4.

57. Ibid., 8.

## Chapter II
## Meeting Mediums... in the Middle

58. Casey, D. (2019, June 6). *The Roanoke Times.*

59. Patton, M. Q. (2002). *Qualitative Evaluation and Research Methods.* (3rd ed.), Thousand Oaks, CA: Sage Publications.

60. Hyman, R. (2003, January/February). How Not to Test Mediums: Critiquing the Afterlife Experiments. *Skeptical Inquire. 27,* 1.

61. Ibid., 254.

62. Bem, D. J. (2005). Review of G. E. Schwartz's *The Afterlife Experiments: Breakthrough Scientific Evidence of Life after Death. Journal of Parapsychology, 69,* 173-183.

63. Anderson, G. and Muir, G. (2017). Blog at Wordpress.com.

64. Martin, J. (2014). Can George Anderson hear the voices of dead people? Retrieved from: https://www.amazon.com/Episode-2/dp/B01MU18HYF/ref=sr_1_5?

65. Ibid.

66. Anderson, G. & Barone, A. (2016). *Life Between Heaven and Earth: What You Didn't Know About the World Hereafter and How It Can Help You.* New York, NY: Harmony Books, 212-213.

67. Caputo, T. (2020). *Good Mourning: Moving Through Everyday Losses with Wisdom from the Other Side.* New York, NY: HarperCollins Publishers, 212-213.

68. Caputo, T. (2013). *There's More to Life Than This: Healing Messages, Remarkable Stories, and Insights About the Other Side.* New York, NY: Simon & Schuster, Inc., 54.

69. Ibid., 116-117.

70. Ibid., 226.

71. Excerpt from *Heaven is Beyond Your Wildest Expectations: Ten True Stories of Experiencing Heaven.*

72. Browne, S. (2000). *Life on the Other Side: A Psychic's Tour of the Afterlife.* New York, Dutton Book, 34.

73. Rand, H. (2020). *Everything You Wanted to Know About the Afterlife: But Were Afraid to Ask.* Hillsboro, OR: Beyond Words, 24.

74. Ibid., 25.

75. Ibid., 26.

76. Browne, S. (2000). *Life on the Other Side: A Psychic's Tour of the Afterlife.* New York, Dutton Book, 52.

77. Ibid., 73.

78. Ibid., 243.

79. Beischel, J. (2015). *Investigating Mediums: A Windbridge Institute Collection,* Tucson, AZ: The Windbridge Institute, LLC, 76-77.

80. Williams, L. (2011). *The Survival of the Soul.* Carlsbad, CA: Hay House, Inc., 14-15.

81. Van Praagh, J. (1997). *Talking to Heaven: A Medium's Message of Life After Death.* New York, NY: Penguin Putnam, Inc., 4-5.

82. Ibid., 35.

83. Ibid., 30-31.

84. Higgins, J. and Bergman, C. (2011). *The Everything Guide to Evidence of the Afterlife; A Scientific Approach to Proving the Existence of Life after Death.* Avon, MA: Adams Media, 142.

85. Ibid., 168, 184.

86. Ibid.

87. Rand, H. (2020). *Everything You Wanted to Know About the Afterlife: But Were Afraid to Ask.* Hillsboro, OR: Beyond Words, 14-15.

88. Higgins, J. and Bergman, C. (2011). *The Everything Guide to Evidence of the Afterlife; A Scientific Approach to Proving the Existence of Life After Death.* Avon, MA: Adams Media, 60.

89. Ibid., 67.

90. Ibid., 68.

91. Spivey, G. and Hymel, D. (2006). *Secrets from God: Your Keys to Heaven/Unlocking the Gates to Personal and Spiritual Enlightenment.* Ojai, CA: G.S. Limited Inc., 3-4.

92. Ibid., 7.

93. Ibid., 293.

# Chapter III
## Exploring Death: The Science Behind Near-Death Experiences

94. Beischel, J. (2015). *Investigating Mediums: A Windbridge Institute Collection,* Tucson, AZ: The Windbridge Institute, LLC, 312.

95. Ibid., 113.

96. Ibid., 160.

97. Ibid.

98. Ibid.

99. Atwater, P.M.H. (2011). *Near-Death Experiences: The Rest of the Story.* Charlottesville, VA: Hampton Roads Publishing Company, Inc.,73.

100. Cain, T. (2021). Are Near-Death Experiences Proof of the Afterlife? Retrieved from: https://www.beawake.com/author/tomcain, 4.

101. Musick, S. (2017). *Life After Heaven: How My Time in Heaven Can Transform Your Life on Earth.* New York, NY: WaterBrook, 182.

102. Alexander, E. (2012). *Proof of Heaven: A Neurosurgeon's Journey into the Afterlife.* New York, NY: Simon & Schuster, Inc., 73, 78-79.

103. Long, J. and Perry, P. (2010). *Evidence of the Afterlife: The Science of Near-Death Experiences.* New York, NY: HarperOne, 67.

104. Brackett, D. (2017, December). Living with Limits: The Continuum of Consciousness. *Journal of Consciousness Exploration & Research, 7,* 11, 1084.

105. Ibid.

106. Ibid.

107. Op. cit., 68.

108. Ibid., 6-7.

109. Ibid., 46-50.

110. Cain, T. (2021). Are Near-Death Experiences Proof of the Afterlife? Retrieved from: https://www.beawake.com/author/tomcain, 10

111. Sosteric, M. (2016, December). Mysticism, Consciousness, Death. *Journal of Consciousness Exploration & Research, 7*, 11, 1112-1113.

112. Carter, C. (2012). *Science and the Afterlife Experience: Evidence for the Immortality of Consciousness.* Rochester, VT: Inner Traditions., xv-xvi.

113. Van Lommel, P. (2010). *Consciousness Beyond Life: The Science of the Near-Death Experience.* New York, NY: HarperOne, 330.

114. Ibid., 346.

115. Ibid., 262.

116. Parnia, S. (2006). *What Happens When We Die: A Groundbreaking Study into the Nature of Life and Death.* Carlsbad, CA: Hay House, Inc., 95.

117. Ibid., 144.

118. Ibid., 150.

119. Nixon, G. (2017, June 9). The Legacy Conference: Report on The Science of Consciousness Conference, LA Jolla, California, 2017. *Journal of Consciousness Studies, 24*, 9-10, 268-269.

120. Ibid.

121. Ibid.

122. Brackett, D. (2017, May). Living with Limits: The Continuum of Consciousness. *Scientific GOD Journal, 8*, 5, 321.

123. Cain, T. (2021). Are Near-Death Experiences Proof of the Afterlife? Retrieved from: https://www.beawake.com/author/tomcain, 8.

124. Cain, T. (2021). What Happens When We Die? Retrieved from: https://www.beawake.com/author/tomcain, 3.

125. Atwater, P.M.H. (2011). *Near-Death Experiences: The Rest of the Story.* Charlottesville, VA: Hampton Roads Publishing Company, Inc., 89-90.

126. Ibid., 26.

127. Ibid., 367-368.

128. Kübler-Ross, E. and Kessler, D. (2005). *On Grief and Grieving: Finding the Meaning of Grief Through the Five Stages of Loss.* New York, NY: Scribner, 107.

129. Ibid., 111-112.

130. Ibid., 108-109.

131. Ibid., 213.

132. Higgins, J. and Bergman, C. (2011). *The Everything Guide to Evidence of the Afterlife; A Scientific Approach to Proving the Existence of Life After Death.* Avon, MA: Adams Media, 100

133. Ibid., 257.

134. Newton, M. (2003). *Journey of Souls: Case Studies of Life Between Lives.* St. Paul, MN: Llewellyn Publications, 5.

135. Ibid., 1.

136. Ibid., 3.

137. Charbonier, J. (2012). *7 Reasons to Believe in the Afterlife: A Doctor Reviews the Case for Consciousness After Death.* Rochester, VT: Inner Traditions, xi.

138. Pearson, P. (2014). *Opening Heaven's Door: Investigating Stories of Life, Death, and What Comes After.* New York, NY: Atria Books, 142.

139. Ibid., 151.

140. Greyson, B. (2021). *After: A Doctor Explores What Near-death Experiences Reveal About Life and Beyond.* New York, NY: St. Martin's Publishing Group, 97.

141. Thonnard, M. et al.. (2013). Characteristics of Near-Death Experiences Memories as Compared to Real and Imagined Events Memories. Retrieved from: https://journals.plos.org/plosone/article?id=10.1371/journal.pone.0057620, 4.

142. Ibid.

143. Pearson, P. (2014). *Opening Heaven's Door: Investigating Stories of Life, Death, and What Comes After.* New York, NY: Atria Books, 152.

144. Ibid., 147.

145. Greyson, B. (2021). *After: A Doctor Explores What Near-Death Experiences Reveal About Life and Beyond.* New York, NY: St. Martin's Publishing Group, 130, 138.

146. Ibid., 119.

147. Cook, R. (2017, May). Theories of Consciousness and Death: Does Consciousness End, Continue, Awaken, or Transform When the Body Dies? *Scientific GOD Journal, 8,* 5, 349.

148. Ibid., 353.

149. Ibid.

150. Ibid., 92.

151. Pearson, P. (2014). *Opening Heaven's Door: Investigating Stories of Life, Death, and What Comes After.* New York, NY: Atria Books, 149, 151.

152. Nelson, K. (2011). *The Spiritual Doorway in the Brain: A Neurologist's Search for the God Experience.* New York, NY: Penguin Group (USA) Inc., 132.

153. Ibid.

154. Ibid., 260.

155. Long, J. and Perry, P. (2016). *God and the Afterlife: The Groundbreaking New Evidence for God and Near-Death Experience.* New York, NY: HarperOne, 9.

156. Ibid., 26.

157. Ibid., 147.

158. Pearson, P. (2014). *Opening Heaven's Door: Investigating Stories of Life, Death, and What Comes After.* New York, NY: Atria Books, 154.

159. Ibid., 161.

160. Miller, B. (2012, July 31). $5 Million Grant Awarded by Private Foundation to Study Immortality. *UCR/Today.*

161. Miller, B. (2016, Winter). Flitting through Eternity. *UCR Magazine.*

162. Eshelman, A. (2016). The Afterlife: Beyond Belief. *International Journal for Philosophy of Religion, 80*:2. 163-183. doi: 10.1007/s11153-016-9565-2.

163. Gray, K. et. al. Of Legacies and Ghosts: Good and Evil People Attain Different Kinds of Immortality.

164. Cain, T. (2021). What Happens When we Die? Retrieved from: https://www.beawake.com/author/tomcain, 3.

165. Quantum Death— "Human Cells Carry Quantum Information That Exists as a Soul." (2020, March 14). Retrieved from: https://dailygalaxy.com/2020/03/quantum-death-human-cells-carry-quantum-information-that-exists, 1.

166. Penrose, R. (2021). Life after death: Soul continues on a QUANTUM level—scientists reveal. Retrieved from: https://www.express.co.uk/science/005845/life-after-death, 2.

167. Ibid., 2-3.

168. Ibid., 3.

169. Quantum Theory Could Explain Life After Death. Retrieved from: https://www.faena.com/aleph/quantum-theory-could-explain-life=after-death

170. Cook, R. (2017, May). Theories of Consciousness and Death: Does Consciousness End, Continue, Awaken, or Transform When the Body Dies? *Scientific GOD Journal, 8,* 5, 355.

171. Quantum Death— "Human Cells Carry Quantum Information That Exists as a Soul." (2020, March 14). Retrieved from: https://dailygalaxy.com/2020/03/quantum-death-human-cells-carry-quantum-information-that-exists, 2-3.

172. Ehlmann, B. (2016, December). The Theory of a Natural Afterlife: A Newfound, Real Possibility for What Awaits Us at Death. *Journal of Consciousness Exploration & Research. 7.* 11, 931-950.

173. Ibid.

174. Ibid.

175. Ibid.

176. Moody, R. A. Book Review. Into the *"Proof of Heaven: A Neurosurgeon's Journey into the Afterlife,"* by Eben Alexander III, MD. Retrieved from: Eternea.com

177. Ibid.

178. Alexander, E. (2012). *Proof of heaven: A Neurosurgeon's Journey into the Afterlife.* New York, NY: Simon & Schuster, Inc.

179. Mays. R. (2013, August 12). *Esquire* Article on Eben Alexander Distorts the Facts.

180. Ibid.

181. Ibid.

182. Ibid.

183. Ibid.

184. Nixon, G. (2016, December). I Killed a Squirrel the Other Day... *Journal of Consciousness Exploration & Research, 7.* 11, iv-xiii

185. Stankovich, R. (2016, December). Does the Consciousness End, Remain Alive, or Transform After Death? *Journal of Consciousness Exploration & Research, 7.* 11, 1036-1050.

186. Ibid.

187. Ibid.

188. Moore, L.E. and Greyson, B. (2017). Characteristics of Memories for Near-Death Experiences. *Consciousness and Cognition, 51,* 121.

189. Freeman, C. (1985, July). Near-Death Experiences: Implications for Medical Personnel. *Occupational Health Nursing,* 355.

190. Excerpt from *Heaven is Beyond Your Wildest Expectations: Ten True Stories of Experiencing Heaven.*

191. Martone, R. (2019, September 10). New Clues Found in Understanding Near-Death Experiences. *Scientific American.*

192. Ibid.

193. Ibid.

194. Cook, R. (2017, May). Theories of Consciousness and Death: Does Consciousness End, Continue, Awaken, or Transform When the Body Dies? *Scientific GOD Journal, 8,* 5, 348-360.

195. D'Souza, D. (2009). *Life After Death: The Evidence.* Washington, DC: Regnery Publishing, Inc., 91, 166, 144, 199.

## Chapter IV
## What is That Light Seen by Many NDEers?

196. Lewis, C.S. (1940). *The Problem of Pain.* San Francisco, CA: HarperCollins Publishers, 39.

197. Royce, B. *Russian Symphony: Thoughts about Tchaikovsky.* Retrieved from: www.tchaikovsky-research.net

198. Excerpt from *Heaven is Beyond Your Wildest Expectations: Ten True Stories of Experiencing Heaven.*

199. Long, J. and Perry, P. (2016). *God and the Afterlife: The Groundbreaking New Evidence for God and Near-Death Experience.* New York, NY: HarperOne, 73, 85.

200. Ibid., 174.

201. Ibid., 193.

202. Ibid., 41.

203. Linn, D., Linn, S., and Linn. M. (2016). *The Gifts of Near-Death experiences: You Don't Have to Die to Experience Your True Home.* Charlottesville, VA: Hampton Roads Publishing Company, Inc., 33.

204. Ibid., 34.

205. Ibid.

206. Long, J. and Perry, P. (2016). *God and the Afterlife: The Groundbreaking New Evidence for God and Near-Death Experience.* New York, NY: HarperOne, 196.

207. Op. cit., 69.

208. Ibid., 35.

209. Ibid.

210. Ibid., 71.

211. Ibid., 72.

212. Benedict, M-T. (2012, December 11). Mellen-Thomas Benedict's Near-Death Experience. Retrieved from: http://www.near-death.com/expereinces/reincarnation04.html

213. Ibid.

214. Ibid.

215. Ibid.

216. Ibid.

217. Freeman, C. (1985, July). Near-Death Experiences: Implications for Medical Personnel. *Occupational Health Nursing*, 355.

218. St. Clair, M. (2019). *Near-Death Experiences: A Historical Exploration from the Ancient World to the Present Day.* London, UK: Amber Books, 111.

219.Swancer, B. (2016, May 25). To Hell and Back: The Dark Side of Near-Death Experiences. Retrieved from: https://mysteriousuniverse.org/2016/05/25, 3.

220. Martin, M. (2005). *The Unexplained Near-Death Experiences.* Mankato, MN: Capstone Press, 16.

221. Ibid., 5-6.

222. Ibid., 7.

223. Wallen, A. (2015, April 22). And Then There Was Light: An Abridged Introduction to Near-Death Experiences. *San Diego CityBeat,* 23.

224. Ibid.

225. Sharp, K. (1995). *After the Light: What I Discovered on the Other Side of Life That Can Change Your World.* New York, NY: William Morrow and Company, Inc., ix, 25.

226. Ibid., 121, 139, 185.

227. Ibid.

228. McVea, C. and Tresniowski, A. (2013). *Waking Up in Heaven: A True story of Brokenness, Heaven, and Life Again.* New York, NY: Howard Books, 13, 15151, 164-167.

## Chapter V
## Lessons to be Learned

229. Brown, E. (2013). *Happier Endings: A Meditation on Life and Death.* New York, NY: Simon & Schuster, Inc., 7.

230. D'Souza, D. (2009). *Life After Death: The Evidence.* Washington, DC: Regnery Publishing, Inc., 64.

231. Kübler-Ross. (1991). *On Life After Death.* Berkeley, CA: Celestial Arts, 30-31.

232. Op. cit., 60.

233. Kübler-Ross. (1969). *On Death and Dying.* New York, NY: Scribner, 268.

234. Op. cit., 60.

235. Op. cit., 276.

236. Kübler-Ross. (1991). *On Life after Death.* Berkeley, CA: Celestial Arts, 10.

237. Op. cit., 150.

238. Rand, H. (2020). *Everything You Wanted to Know About the Afterlife: But Were Afraid to Ask.* Hillsboro, OR: Beyond Words, 20.

239. Van Lommel, P. (2010). *Consciousness Beyond Life: The Science of the Near-Death Experience.* New York, NY: HarperOne, 68.

240. Greyson, B. (2021). *After: A Doctor Explores What Near-Death Experiences Reveal About Life and Beyond.* New York, NY: St. Martin's Publishing Group, 216-221.

241. Ibid., 223.

242. Freeman, C. (1985, July). Near-Death Experiences: Implications for Medical Personnel. *Occupational Health Nursing*, 358.

243. Ibid.

244. Ibid., 353.

245. St. Clair, M. (2019). *Near-Death Experiences: A Historical Exploration from the Ancient World to the Present Day.* London, UK: Amber Books, 93, 114.

246. Long, J. (2014, September-October). Near-Death Experiences Evidence for Their Reality. *Missouri Medicine, 111*(5), 372-380.

247. Cahn, J. (2016). *The Book of Mysteries.* Lake Mary, FL: FrontLine, 288, 316, 360.

## Chapter VI
## "I" Witnesses

248. Palmateer, J. (2008, January 22). Bolt Leads to Key Moment. Retrieved from: hyyp://thedailystar.com/local/x112892347/Bolt-leads-to-key-moment

249. Henig, R. M. (2016, April). The Crossing. *National Geographic, 229*, 4, 30-52.

250. Martin, M. (2005). *The Unexplained Near-Death Experiences.* Mankato, MN: Capstone Press, 8.

251. Ibid., 16.

## Chapter VII
## Conclusions

252. Kerr, C. and Mardorossian, C. (2020). *Death is but a Dream: Finding Hope and Meaning at Life's End.* New York, NY: Penguin Random House, 227-228.

253. Brown, E. (2013). *Happier Endings: A Meditation on Life and Death.* New York, NY: Simon & Schuster, Inc., 260.

254. Ibid., 265.

255. Ibid., 294.

256. Lewis, C.S. (1940). *The Problem of Pain.* San Francisco, CA: HarperCollins Publishers, 47.

257. Pearson, P. (2014). *Opening Heaven's Door: Investigating Stories of Life, Death, and What Comes After.* New York, NY: Atria Books, 149.

258. Nelson, K. (2011). *The Spiritual Doorway in the Brain: A Neurologist's Search for the God Experience.* New York, NY: Penguin Group (USA) Inc., 260.

259. Ibid., 261.

260. Ibid., 132.

261. Ibid.

262. Op. cit., 161-162.

263. Pearson, P. (2014). *Opening Heaven's Door: Investigating Stories of Life, Death, and What Comes After.* New York, NY: Atria Books, 161.0

264. Moore, L.E. and Greyson, B. (2017). Characteristics of Memories for Near-Death Experiences. *Consciousness and Cognition, 51,* 123.

265. Van Lommel, P. (2010). *Consciousness Beyond Life: The Science of the Near-Death Experience.* New York, NY: HarperOne, 149.

266. Long, J. (2014, September-October). Near-Death Experiences Evidence for Their Reality. *Missouri Medicine, 111*(5), 372-380.

267. Isaacson, W. (2011). *Steve Jobs.* New York, NY: Simon & Schuster, 457.

268. Jobs, S. (2005, June 12). Commencement Address at Stanford University. Retrieved from: http://news.stanford.edu/news/2005/june15/jobs-061505.html

269. Op. cit., 571.

270. Stetzer, E. (2011, October). Remarkable Thoughts on Death from Steve Jobs. Retrieved from: https://www.christianitytoday.com/edstetzer/2011/october/remarkable-thoughts-on-death-from-steve-jobs.html

271. Ibid.

272. Ibid.

273. Miller, I. (2017, May). The Mask of Eternity: The Quest for Immortality and the Afterlife. *Scientific GOD Journal, 8,* 5, 406.

274. Ibid.

275. Ibid., 413.

276. Freeman, C. (1985, July). Near-Death Experiences: Implications for Medical Personnel. *Occupational Health Nursing,* 352.

277. Ibid., 357.

278. Ibid., 358.

279. Cahn, J. (2014). *The Mystery of the Shemitah.* Lake Mary, Fl: FrontLine, 4.

280. Ibid., 248.

281. Ring, K. (1999). Retrieved from Near Death Experience Research Foundation (www.nderf.org).

282. Panagore, P. (2015). *Heaven is Beautiful: How Dying Taught Me That Death is Just the Beginning.* Charlottesville, VA: Hampton Roads Publishing Company, Inc., 80.

283. Ibid., 81.

284. Ibid., 85-86.

285. Ibid., 189.

286. Excerpt from Morse, M. and Perry. P. (1990*). Closer to the Light: Learning from Near Death Experiences of Children.* New York, NY: Villard Books.

# References

✓ Indicates recommended reading of individuals' personal NDEs

Albom, M. (2003). *The Five People You Meet in Heaven.* New York, NY: Hyperion.

Alexander, E. (2012). *Proof of Heaven: A Neurosurgeon's Journey into the Afterlife.* New York, NY: Simon & Schuster, Inc.

Anderson, G. and Barone, A. (2016). *Life Between Heaven and Earth: What You Didn't Know About the World Hereafter and How It Can Help You.* New York, NY: Harmony Books.

Anderson, G. and Muir, G. (2017). Blog at Wordpress.com.

Atwater, P. M. H. (2011). *Near-Death Experiences: The Rest of the Story.* Charlottesville, VA: Hampton Roads Publishing Company, Inc.

Atwater, P. M. H. (2007). *The Big Book of Near-Death Experiences: The Ultimate Guide to What Happens When We Die.* Charlottesville, VA: Hampton Roads Publishing Company, Inc.

✓ Bascom, L. and Loecher, B. (1995). *By the Light.* New York, NY: Avon Books.

Beischel, J. (2015). *Investigating Mediums: A Windbridge Institute Collection,* Tucson, AZ: The Windbridge Institute, LLC.

Bem, D. J. (2005). Review of G. E. Schwartz's *The Afterlife Experiments: Breakthrough Scientific Evidence of Life after Death. Journal of Parapsychology, 69,* 173-183.

Benedict, M-T. (2012, December 11). Mellen-Thomas Benedict's Near-Death Experience. Retrieved from: http://www.near-death.com/expereinces/reincarnation04.html

Besteman, M. and Craker, L. (2012). *My Journey to Heaven: What I Saw and How It Changed My Life*. Grand Rapids, MI: Revell.

Beuregard, M. and O'Leary, D. (2007). *The Spiritual Brain: A Neuroscientist's Case for the Existence of the Soul*. New York, NY: HarperCollins Publishers.

✓ Bence, E., ed. (2008). *Comfort from Beyond: Real-life Experiences of Hope in the Face of Loss*. New York, NY: Guideposts.
✓ Black, D. (2010). *Flight to Heaven: A Pilot's True Story*. Bloomington, MN: Bethany House Publishers.

Brackett, D. (2017, May). Living with Limits: The Continuum of Consciousness. *Scientific GOD Journal, 8*, 5, 305-325.

Brackett, D. (2016, December). Living with Limits: The Continuum of Consciousness. *Journal of Consciousness Exploration & Research, 7*, 11, 1078-1098.

Brown, E. (2013). *Happier Endings: A Meditation on Life and Death*. New York, NY: Simon & Schuster, Inc.

Browne, S. (2011). *Afterlives of the Rich and Famous*. New York, NY: HarperOne.

Browne, S. (2000). *Life on the Other Side: A Psychic's Tour of the Afterlife*. New York, Dutton Book.

✓ Burpo, T. (2010*). Heaven is for Real: A Little Boy's Astounding Story of His Trip to Heaven and Back*. Nashville, TN: Thomas Nelson.

Cahn, J. (2016). *The Book of Mysteries*. Lake Mary, FL: FrontLine.

Cain, T. (2021). Are Near-Death Experiences Proof of the Afterlife? Retrieved from: https://www.beawake.com/author/tomcain

Cain, T. (2021). What Happens When We Die? Retrieved from: https://www.beawake.com/author/tomcain

Caputo, T. (2020). *Good Mourning: Moving Through Everyday Losses with Wisdom from the Other Side*. New York, NY: HarperCollins Publishers.

Caputo, T. (2017). *Good Grief: Heal Your Soul, Honor Your Loved Ones, and Learn to Live Again*. New York, NY: Simon & Schuster, Inc.

Caputo, T. (2013). *There's More to Life Than This: Healing Messages, Remarkable Stories, and Insights About the Other Side*. New York, NY: Simon & Schuster, Inc.

Carter, C. (2012). *Science and the Afterlife Experience: Evidence for the Immortality of Consciousness*. Rochester, VT: Inner Traditions.

Carter, C. (2010). *Science and the Near-Death Experience: How Consciousness Survives Death*. Rochester, VT: Inner Traditions.

Casey, D. (2019, June 6). *The Roanoke Times*.

Caudill, M. (2012). *Impossible Realities: The Science Behind Energy Healing, Telepathy, Reincarnation, Precognition, and Other Black Swan Phenomena*. Charlottesville, VA: Hampton Roads Publishing Company, Inc.

Charbonier, J. (2012). *7 Reasons to Believe in the Afterlife: A Doctor Reviews the Case for Consciousness after Death.* Rochester, VT: Inner Traditions.

Cook, E., Greyson, B., and Stevenson, I. (1998). Do Any Near-Death Experiences Provide Evidence for the Survival of Human Personality After Death? Relevant Features and Illustrative Case Reports. *Journal of Scientific Exploration, 12*(3), 377-406.

Cook, R. (2017, May). Theories of Consciousness and Death: Does Consciousness End, Continue, Awaken, or Transform When the Body Dies? *Scientific GOD Journal, 8*, 5, 348-360.

Dale, C. (2013). *The Journey after Life: What Happens When We Die.* Boulder, CO: Sounds True, Inc.

Dittrich, L. (2013, August). The Prophet. *Esquire, 160,* 1, 89-95, 125-128.

Donne, J. *Death be not proud.* Retrieved from: https://www.litcharts.com

D'Souza, D. (2009). *Life after Death: The Evidence.* Washington, DC: Regnery Publishing, Inc.

Ehlmann, B. (2016, December). The Theory of a Natural Afterlife: A Newfound, Real Possibility for What Awaits Us at Death. *Journal of Consciousness Exploration & Research. 7.* 11, 931-950.

Eshelman, A. (2016). The Afterlife: Beyond Belief. *International Journal for Philosophy of Religion, 80*:2. 163-183. doi: 10.1007/s11153-016-9565-2.

✓ Gavlak, L. *Modern Day Miracles: Miraculous True Life Encounters.* Kylertown, PA: LJ GavlakPublishing.

Freeman, C. (1985, July). Near-Death Experiences: Implications for Medical Personnel. *Occupational Health Nursing*, 349-359.

Gray, K. et. al. Of Legacies and Ghosts: Good and Evil People Attain Different Kinds of Immortality.

Greyson, B. (2021). *After: A Doctor Explores What Near-Death Experiences Reveal About Life and Beyond.* New York, NY: St. Martin's Publishing Group.

Henig, R. M. (2016, April). The Crossing. *National Geographic, 229,* 4, 30-52.

Hensley, M. (2015). *Promised by Heaven: A Doctor's Return from the Afterlife to a Destiny of Love and Healing.* New York, NY: Simon & Schuster, Inc.

Higgins, J. and Bergman, C. (2011). *The Everything Guide to Evidence of the Afterlife; A Scientific Approach to Proving the Existence of Life After Death.* Avon, MA: Adams Media.

*Holy Bible, New King James Version.* 1982. Nashville, TN: Thomas Nelson, Inc.

Horowitz, L. (2000). *Healing Celebrations: Miraculous Recoveries Through Ancient Scriptures, Natural Medicine and Modern Science.* Sandpoint, ID: Tetrahedron Publishing Group.

Hyman, R. (2003, January/February). How Not to Test Mediums: Critiquing the Afterlife Experiments. *Skeptical Inquire. 27,* 1.

Jeremiah, D. (2014). *Agents of the Apocalypse: A Riveting Look at the Key Players of the End Times.* Carol Stream, Il: Tyndale House Publishers, Inc., 207.

Jobs, S. (2005, June 12). Commencement Address at Stanford University. Retrieved from: http://news.stanford.edu/news/2005/june15/jobs-061505.html

John, T. (2015). *Never Argue with a Dead Person: True and Unbelievable Stories from the Other Side.* Charlottesville, VA: Hampton Roads Publishing Company, Inc.

*Journal of Consciousness Exploration & Research: Theories of Consciousness and Death.* (2016, December). *7.* 11, 992-1011.

Kaiser, S. (2015). *Adventures for Your Soul: 21 Ways to Transform Your Habits and Reach Your Full Potential.* New York, NY: Berkley Books.

Kerr, C. and Mardorossian, C. (2020). *Death is But a Dream: Finding Hope and Meaning at Life's End.* New York, NY: Penguin Random House.

Kessler, D. (2010). *Visions, Trips, and Crowded Rooms: Who and What You See Before You Die.* Carlsbad, CA: Hay House, Inc.

✓ Kopecky, R. (2014). *How to Survive Life (and Death): A Guide for Happiness in This World and Beyond.* San Francisco, CA: Conari Press.

Kragen, P. (2014, March 19). Death Cafes Talk Up Dying. *San Diego Union Tribune.*

Kübler-Ross, E. (1969). *On Death and Dying.* New York, NY: Scribner.

Kübler-Ross, E. (1991). *On Life After Death.* Berkeley, CA: Celestial Arts.

Kübler-Ross, E. and Kessler, D. (2005). *On Grief and Grieving: Finding the Meaning of Grief Through the Five Stages of Loss.* New York, NY: Scribner.

*The Lazarus Phenomenon: A Glimpse of Eternity.* (2009). Worldwide Media. Distributed by Total-Content LLC.

Lesslie, R. (2014). *Miracles in the ER.* Eugene, OR: Harvest House Publishers.

Lesslie, R. (2012). *Angles on the Nightshift: Inspirational True Stories from the ER.* Eugene, OR: Harvest House Publishers.

Levitt, A. (2013, July 11). Heaven Can't Wait: A Skeptic's Guide to Afterlife Awareness. *The Riverfront Times.*

Lewis, C. S. (1940). *The Problem of Pain.* San Francisco, CA: HarperCollins Publishers.

Linn, D., Linn, S., and Linn. M. (2016). *The Gifts of Near-Death Experiences: You Don't Have to Die to Experience Your True Home.* Charlottesville, VA: Hampton Roads Publishing Company, Inc.

Long, J. (2014, September-October). Near-Death Experiences Evidence for Their Reality. *Missouri Medicine, 111*(5), 372-380.

Long, J. and Perry, P. (2010). *Evidence of the Afterlife: The Science of Near-Death Experiences.* New York, NY: HarperOne.

Long, J. and Perry, P. (2016). *God and the Afterlife: The Groundbreaking New Evidence for God and Near-Death Experience.* New York, NY: HarperOne.

✓ Malarkey, K. and Malarkey, A. (2011). *The Boy Who Came Back from Heaven: Remarkable Account of Miracles, Angels, and Life Beyond This World.* Carol Stream, IOL: Tyndale House Publishers, Inc.

Mann, D. and Becker, K. (2020*). Facing Your Fears: A Navy Seal's Guide to Coping with Fear and Anxiety.* New York, NY: Skyhorse Publishing.

Martin, J. (2014). Can George Anderson Hear the Voices of Dead People? Retrieved from: https://www.amazon.com/Episode-2/dp/B01MU18HYF/ref=sr_1_5?

Martin, M. (2005). *The Unexplained Near-Death Experiences.* Mankato, MN: Capstone Press.

Martone, R. (2019, September 10). New Clues Found in Understanding Near-Death Experiences. *Scientific American.*

Mays. R. (2013, August 12). *Esquire* Article on Eben Alexander Distorts the Facts.

✓ McVea, C. and Tresniowski, A. (2013). *Waking Up in Heaven: A True Story of Brokenness, Heaven, and Life Again.* New York, NY: Howard Books.

Miller, B. (2016, Winter). Flitting Through Eternity. *UCR Magazine.*

Miller, B. (2012, July 31). $5 Million Grant Awarded by Private Foundation to Study Immortality. *UCR/Today.*

Miller, I. (2017, May). The Mask of Eternity: The Quest for Immortality and the Afterlife. *Scientific GOD Journal, 8*, 5, 405-415.

Mirabello, M. (2016). *A Traveler's Guide to the Afterlife: Traditions and Beliefs on Death, Dying, and What Lies Beyond.* Rochester, VT: Inner Traditions.

Moody, R. A. Book Review. Into the *"Proof of Heaven: A Neurosurgeon's Journey into the Afterlife,"* by Eben Alexander III, MD. Retrieved from: Eternea.com

Moody, R. and Perry, P. (2012). *Paranormal: My Life in Pursuit of the Afterlife.* New York, NY: HarperCollins Publishers.

Moody, R. and Perry, P. (201). *Glimpses of Eternity: Sharing a Loved One's Passage from This Life to the Next.* New York, NY: Guideposts.

Moore, L.E. and Greyson, B. (2017). Characteristics of Memories for Near-Death Experiences. *Consciousness and Cognition, 51,* 116-124.

Moorjani, A. (2012). *Dying to Be Me: My Journey from Cancer, to Near Death, to True Healing.* Carlsbad, CA: Hay House, Inc.

Morse, M. and Perry. P. (1990*). Closer to the Light: Learning from Near Death Experiences of Children.* New York, NY: Villard Books.

✓ Moss, R. (2014). *The Boy Who Died and Came Back: Adventures of a Dream Archaeologist in the Multiverse.* Novato, CA: New World Library.

Musick, S. (2017). *Life After Heaven: How My Time in Heaven Can Transform Your Life on Earth.* New York, NY: WaterBrook.

✓ Near Death Experience Research Foundation (www.nderf.org). As of August 18, 2021, 4,945 exceptional NDEs are detailed, as well as 4,949 current NDEs.

Nelson, K. (2011). *The Spiritual Doorway in the Brain: A Neurologist's Search for the God Experience.* New York, NY: Penguin Group (USA) Inc.

Newton, M. (2003). *Destiny of Souls: New Case Studies of Life Between Lives.* St. Paul, MN: Llewellyn Publications.

Newton, M. (2003). *Journey of Souls: Case Studies of Life Between Lives.* St. Paul, MN: Llewellyn Publications.

Nixon, G. (2016, December). I Killed a Squirrel the Other Day… *Journal of Consciousness Exploration & Research, 7.* 11, iv-xiii

Nixon, G. (2017, June 9). The Legacy Conference: Report on the Science of Consciousness Conference, La Jolla, California, 2017. *Journal of Consciousness Studies, 24,* 9-10, 268-269.

Palmateer, J. (2008, January 22). Bolt Leads to Key Moment. Retrieved from: hyyp://thedailystar.com/local/x112892347/Bolt-leads-to-key-moment

Panagore, P. (2015). *Heaven is Beautiful: How Dying Taught Me That Death is Just the Beginning.* Charlottesville, VA: Hampton Roads Publishing Company, Inc.

Parnia, S. (2006). *What Happens When We Die: A Groundbreaking Study into the Nature of Life and Death.* Carlsbad, CA: Hay House, Inc.

Parti, R. (2016). *Dying to Wake Up: A Doctor's Voyage into the Afterlife and the Wisdom He Brought Back.* New York, NY: Atria Books.

✓ Paters, V. and Schuelke, C. (2015). *Heaven is a Breath Away: An Unexpected Journey to Heaven and Back.* New York, NY: Guideposts.

Patton, M. Q. (2002). *Qualitative Evaluation and Research Methods.* (3$^{rd}$ ed.), Thousand Oaks, CA: Sage Publications.

Pearson, P. (2014). *Opening Heaven's Door: Investigating Stories of Life, Death, and What Comes After.* New York, NY: Atria Books.

Penrose, R. (2021). Life After Death: Soul Continues on a QUANTUM Level—Scientists Reveal. Retrieved from: https://www.express.co.uk/science/005845/life-after-death

✓ Piper, D. (2004). *90 Minutes in Heaven: A True Story of Death and Life.* Grand Rapids, MI: Baker Publishing Group.

Quantum death— "Human Cells Carry Quantum Information That Exists as a Soul." (2020, March 14). Retrieved from: https://dailygalaxy.com/2020/03/quantum-death-human-cells-carry-quantum-information-that-exists

Quantum Theory Could Explain Life After Death. Retrieved from: https://www.faena.com/aleph/quantum-theory-could-explain-life=after-death

Rand, H. (2020). *Everything You Wanted to Know About the Afterlife: But Were Afraid to Ask.* Hillsboro, OR: Beyond Words.

✓ Ritchie, G. (2007). *Return from Tomorrow.* Grand Rapids, MI: Baker Publishing Group.

✓ Robinson, M. (2014). *Falling into Heaven: A Skydiver's Gripping Account of Heaven, Healing, and Miracles.* Racine, WI: Broadstreet Publishing Group, LLC.

✓ Roth, S. and Lane, L. (2012). *Heaven is Beyond Your Wildest Expectations: Ten True Stories of Experiencing Heaven.* Shippensburg, PA: Destiny Image Publishers, Inc.

✓ Sherrill, E. (2002). *All the Way to Heaven: A Surprising Faith Journal.* Grand Rapids, MI: Baker Book House Company.

✓ Sigmund, R. (2010). *My Time in Heaven: A True Story of Dying...and Coming Back.* New Kensington, PA: Whitaker House.

Ring, K. (1999). The Greatest Gift. Near Death Experience Research Foundation (www.nderf.org).

Rock, A., Beischel, J., and Schwartz, G. (2009, Fall). Is There Madness in our Mediumship Methods? A Response to Roxburgh and Roe. *Journal of Scientific Research, 23,* (3).

✓ Roth, S. and Lane, L. (2012). *Heaven Is Beyond Your Wildest Expectations: Ten True Stories of Experiencing Heaven.* Shippensburg, PA: Destiny Publishing, Inc.

St. Clair, M. (2019). *Near-Death Experiences: A Historical Exploration from the Ancient World to the Present Day.* London, UK: Amber Books.

*Scientific GOD Journal: Exploration of Life After Death.* (2017, May). *8,* 5, 293-421.

Sharp, K. (1995). *After the Light: What I Discovered on the Other Side of Life That Can Change Your World.* New York, NY: William Morrow and Company, Inc.

Sosteric, M. (2016, December). Mysticism, Consciousness, Death. *Journal of Consciousness Exploration & Research, 7,* 11, 1099-1118.

Spivey, G. and Hyel, D. (2006). *Secrets from God: Your Keys to Heaven/Unlocking the Gates to Personal and Spiritual Enlightenment.* Ojai, CA: G.S. Limited Inc.

Stankovich, R. (2016, December). Does the Consciousness End, Remain Alive, or Transform After Death? *Journal of Consciousness Exploration & Research, 7.* 11, 1036-1050.

Stetzer, E. (2011, October). Remarkable Thoughts on Death from Steve Jobs. Retrieved from: https://www.christianitytoday.com/edstetzer/2011/october/remarkable-thoughts-on-death-from-steve-jobs.html

Stone, A. (2011). *The Unexplained: Near-Death Experiences.* Minneapolis, MN: Bellwether Media.

Strong, J. (1990). *The New Strong's Exhaustive Concordance of the Bible.* Nashville, TN: Thomas Nelson Publishers.

Swancer, B. (2016, May 25). To Hell and Back: The Dark Side of Near-Death Experiences. Retrieved from: https;//mysteriousuniverse.org/2016/05/25

Swindoll, C. (1998). *The Tale of the Tardy Oxcart and 1501 Other Stories.* Dallas, TX: Word, 183.

Thomas, D. *Do Not Go Gentle Into That Good Night.* Retrieved from: https://www.litcharts.com

Thonnard, M. et al. (2013). Characteristics of Near-Death Experiences Memories as Compared to Real and Imagined Events Memories. Retrieved from: https://journals.plos.org/plosone/article?id=10.1371/journal.pone.0057620

Timmerman, T. (2015). Why Lament a Bad Death." *The Philosophers' Magazine, 69*:44-50. doi: 10.540/tpm20156941.

Tompkins, P. (2012). *The Modern Book of the Dead: A Revolutionary Perspective on Death, the Soul, and What Really Happens in the Life to Come.* New York, NY: Atria Books.

Tripp, R. T. (1970). *The International Thesaurus of Quotations.* New York, NY: Harper & Row, Publishers, Inc.

Van Lommel, P. (2010). *Consciousness Beyond Life: The Science of the Near-Death Experience.* New York, NY: HarperOne.

Van Praagh, J. (1997). *Talking to Heaven: A Medium's Message of Life After Death.* New York, NY: Penguin Putnam, Inc.

Van Praag, J. (2009). *Unfinished Business: What the Dead Can Teach Us About Life.* New York, NY: HarperOne.

Van Praagh, J. (2011). *Growing Up in Heaven: The Eternal Connection Between Parent and Child.* New York, NY: HarperOne.

Wallen, A. (2015, April 22). And Then There Was Light: An Abridged Introduction to Near-Death Experiences. *San Diego CityBeat, 23.*

Weschcke, C. and Slate, J. (2011). *The Llewellyn Complete Book of Psychic Empowerment: A Compendium of Tools & Techniques for Growth & Transformation.* St. Woodbury, MN: Llewellyn Publications.

Williams, L. (2011). *The Survival of the Soul.* Carlsbad, CA: Hay House, Inc.

✓ Zukav, G. (1989). *The Seat of the Soul: 25ᵗʰ Anniversary Edition.* New York, NY: Simon & Schuster, Inc.

# ABOUT THE AUTHOR

## Joseph F. Cortese, Ed.D.

Widener University, Chester, PA
Doctor of Education, Educational Leadership, 2008.

Widener University, Chester, PA
Master of Education, Educational Leadership, 2000
Principal Certification, K-12, Superintendent's Letter of Eligibility, 2000.

Carlow University, Pittsburgh, PA
15 credits, Positive and Assertive Discipline, 1994.

Lehigh University, Bethlehem, PA
Master of Arts, Secondary Education, 1978.

East Stroudsburg University, East Stroudsburg, PA
Bachelor of Science in Secondary English, 1973
Minors: Special Education, German, and Social Studies.

World Christianship Ministries, Fresno, CA
Doctor of Divinity, 2008 (Honorary).
Ordained as an independent Christian clergy and Pastoral Counselor, 2012.

# MAIL-ORDER PAGE

++++++++++++++++++++++++++++++++++++++++++++++++

## Send order page, along with check or money order to:

Dr. Joseph F. Cortese

951 Las Palmas Entrada Ave. Apt. 1328

Henderson, NV 89012

**Shipping address: (PLEASE PRINT)**

Name:
_____

Address:
_____

City, State, Zip:
_____

Telephone (optional):
_____

E-mail (optional):
_____

| Book Title | Price | Quantity | Subtotal |
|:---:|:---:|:---:|:---:|
| *Phoenixivity* | 10.00 | | |
| *The Missing Link in American Public Education* | 15.00 | | |
| *After We Die, Then What?* | 20.00 | | |
| (Shipping and handling included) | **Total:** | | |